Smoke

*An Anthology of Work from the
CreativeWriting Programme at the
University of Gloucestershire*

Edited by D.D. Johnston & Tyler Keevil

Poetry edited by Daniel Sluman & Lucy Tyler

First Published 2012 by Templar Poetry
For Horseplay Press
Fenelon House,
Kingsbridge Terrace,
Dale Road, Matlock, Derbyshire
DE4 3NB

ISBN 978-1-906285-41-8
Copyright © Editors and Contributors 2012
The Prose Editors D.D. Johnston & Tyler Keevil,
The Poetry Editors Daniel Sluman & Lucy Tyler
&
The Contributors have asserted their rights to be identified
As the authors of this work in accordance
With the Copyright, Designs and Patents Act 1988.

For permission to reprint or broadcast these poems write to
Templar Poetry
A CIP catalogue record of this book is available
From the British Library.
Typeset by Pliny
Graphics by Pliny
Printed and Bound in India

Contents

Prose

Editorial

Smoke: A Creative Writing Anthology

This new collection of undergraduate and postgraduate writing was conceived in the summer of 2011, against a backdrop of Arab revolutions, urban riots, strikes, protests, and financial collapse. It is being edited in the summer of 2012, when, in Cheltenham at least, union flag bunting hangs across sleepy side streets, and newspapers celebrate a hereditary monarch and the slow pilgrimage of a faltering torch. It's a reminder how quickly things change: a nod to the power of culture and the world's new speed.

How are we writers to keep up? Every year there are new fashions, new cultures, new hatreds, new attitudes, new technologies, and new ways of living. Fortunately, every year, there are also new voices emerging to make sense of it all. This anthology contains thirty-three new voices: a selection from the many talented students at The University of Gloucestershire.

Some of the writers featured in *Smoke* have already had publishing success elsewhere; for many of them, however, this is the first time they have thrown their work out into our uncertain world. Some of them may never publish again. They will devote their lives to other pursuits in other fields and their education will be no less useful for it. The Creative Writing degrees at the University of Gloucestershire teach much more than how to sell stories; they are spaces in which students also develop their critical thinking, problem solving, and empathy – skills our world urgently needs.

For others, however, this will be their first of many publications. These are writers with time and talent on their side, who will entertain us, make us think, and help to shape our culture. Remember: you read them here first.

D.D. Johnston & Tyler Keevil
June 2012

Prose

Old Sword / *Tatia Nichols-Arlès*

Mostly I remember the green grass of 1973 and that Nina and I were mad for gymnastics. Nadia Comaneci and Olga Korbut were the darlings of the summer Olympics and we were their disciples, in our Woodstock and Snoopy T-shirts and our yellow terry-cloth shorts with thick orange piping around the seams; we would practice our summersaults, cartwheels, round-offs and handstands. Nina was younger and more flexible and, at age four, could tumble and stand on her hands with ease. My arms got tired after a while but my round-offs were better. Nothing felt so good as landing a good round-off: straight legs snapping closed like a switchblade, the thrill of landing and the accompanying little bounce after you nailed it. We worked hard to win our gold and silver medals in that front yard.

It must have been the sight of us doing handstands that attracted him. Those golden girl thighs, spread-eagled to the sky, as we held each other's ankles, laughing while our heads filled with blood. I don't know how long it was before I noticed the car, lingering there by the curb, with its engine running: something new in the neighbourhood. It beckoned us. The car window was open and a man waved before driving up the street and pulling to the curb again in front of our neighbours' house. We followed. We didn't go right up to the window, but stood on the sidewalk. The man said hi. He had a nice smile. Even now I remember it as the kind of warm smile that reassures and can be trusted. I had good instincts, still do, and I knew this man wasn't going to do us harm. There were two of us, we could run fast, and our house was behind us with Mom inside. We weren't afraid. We were definitely not getting in his car. I knew that much.

The man said hi and asked us our names. He guessed we were sisters. We laughed when he thought I was the younger one because I was so much taller. The man wanted to know what we were doing on such a nice day. We told him about playing gymnastics. He knew all about Nadia and Olga, and we showed him all of our best routines there on Mr and Mrs Patterson's yard. Though we lived in the neighbourhood for years, they never seemed to be there. At least that's how I remember it. In fact, there was no one around on South A Street on a hot, sunny day in the 1970s. This was before missing person milk cartons. Before Summer, a local three-year-old girl, was abducted and murdered, her body dumped in the Willamette River, not to be discovered until years later.

This man was kind and liked our shirts. He had two boys who were about our age.

'Come closer if you want to,' he said. 'I'm not going to hurt you,' and he held up two fingers for the Scout salute. I believed him. I was a Girl Scout too. Even now, when I recall his face, it seems trustworthy. We went right up to the window.

The man had one hand on the steering wheel and one hand between his legs, rubbing his dick. I had only seen a penis a few times before: once when Lee Lockwood made me pull down my pants then pulled his down and made me touch it. I didn't want to but he said he would hit me and tell my Mom, so I did. And the occasional brief glimpses of my Dad's. Dad didn't seem to want me to see his. Once when I heard a strange sound, I went into my parents' bedroom and saw my Dad on top of my Mom going up and down. 'Hey, get out of here!' he yelled. I bolted, confused and frightened. Later, I had to stand in the corner as punishment. So the appendage between my Dad's legs – his penis – became this forbidden thing, and it made me curious.

This man's penis was the first one I had seen close up. It was erect, circumcised and looked like a purple swollen mushroom. It reminded me of mushroom picking in the woods with my Mom's friend Marcia. She was a mushroom expert. She and my Mom used to get so excited over all the different varieties they found. Nina and I would pretend to be interested for a while but eventually we'd get fed up and climb trees instead. On the way back home, we'd look at all the different kinds of mushrooms they collected. The man's penis was a big tall one. It could have been like one of the others in their basket.

'Do you mind if I do this while you're here?' the man asked. 'It just makes me feel better when I rub it,' and he continued to stroke himself up and down, up and down. 'I'm going to drive around the block,' he said. 'Do you want to follow?' We followed. This was far more interesting than gymnastics. 'I'd let you touch it but I don't want anyone to see,' he said. 'Do you want to touch it?' he asked.

'Okay.' We did. Of course we did, like we wanted to touch a pony or a snake. It was irresistible. The man pulled the car into the alley and we touched it. It felt velvety and soft, like a kitten's belly – nothing like Lee Lockwood's. I knew we were doing a bad thing but we didn't stop. At some point, I took note of his license plate. Why, when I was participating, I don't know. Perhaps that's what makes it so painful to remember. Even now, I wonder if it was wrong to let it carry on so long. Why didn't we run when we first saw his trousers open and his hand on his dick? Maybe that's why I got the license number, some kind of redemption.

We followed him around the block for what seemed like ages, but was probably only twenty minutes. After a while, we got bored with his penis and decided to play drive-thru. He played along beautifully, ordering loads of food, pretending to pay us after we gave him his bags. We played McDonald's and Taco Bell too. All the while, the man rubbed himself; sometimes fast, sometimes slow. At one point, he drove off, but he came back. We made sure to give him the change from his order. Eventually he said he had to go, but he would come again sometime. Then the man drove away.

When we eventually went inside, I casually mentioned our game with the man. I remember my Mom's sharp look as she gazed at me, like something under a microscope, and she wanted to know everything that had happened. I told her what I could remember, including the license plate number and the make of the car. I knew it was an Olds Cutlass because my Grandpa had one too. He called it his old sword.

Police detectives came to the house to interview my sister and me that day. They asked us loads of questions and because I was older and more aware, I had to answer them. Nina was frightened and just froze up. The questions kept coming – a child grilling:

'What did he look like?'

'What was he wearing?'

'What did he say?'

'Did he touch you?'

Sometimes they repeated the same questions in different ways, like they wanted to trip me up or something. The detectives were frighteningly official, and I was sure I was in trouble for touching this man's penis. My stomach began to cramp. They wanted to know why we followed him into the alley. I didn't know what to say; I knew I couldn't say because I wanted to touch it. There was such an air of censure in the room. I can still feel the way my skin crawled with shame. Touching a penis must have been wrong, and I should never do it again. Though secretly, I was glad that I had gotten to see and touch the man's penis before I told my Mom and the other girls in my class.

The one thing I seemed to have done right was to memorise the license plate number. All the adults were pleased about that. Finally the interrogation was over. They told us we might have to tell the story again in court, and asked us if that would be okay? I wasn't too sure what 'court' was, but I would have said yes to anything those police people asked. They left their card with my Mom and told her to call them if anyone saw the man again.

I was relieved it was over. My stomach ache eased and Mom must have felt we'd been through enough because she made us chocolate chip cookies while we watched cartoons. I never wanted to go outside again. When my Dad got home from work, she told him about the whole thing in the kitchen. I heard him shout and hit the table and it set my stomach off again. Then they both came into the living room and turned off the TV, right in the middle of Popeye. I knew it was going to be serious. They told us we were not to talk to anyone we didn't know, unless they, or some other adult we knew, was with us. That we should never touch a person's privates or let anyone else touch our private places either. I wanted to ask them why they touched their private places together. But I didn't. I wanted to ask if it was okay if Grandpa tickled me in my private places or if Nina and I could touch each other's privates. But I didn't. I didn't dare ask anything. They turned the TV back on and we never talked about the man or his penis again.

Sometime later, I heard my Mom on the phone telling the story of the man and his car to a friend. She said that one of the detectives had called and told her the man had been caught and arrested.

'He confessed everything, thank god, so the girls won't have to testify. Apparently he's done this type of thing before, the sick bastard. And you're not going to believe this: not only is he married with two kids, but he's a Pastor in a church!'

Then Mom laughed and said, 'Yeah, Jesus Christ is right!'

Before You Pay the Rent / *Luke Dean*

I've recently started to work in an office. All the phones sound far away, even the one at my desk. The guy next to me, Simon, will do well. He doesn't panic when the calls page gets full and he knows how to talk to people. I can't think what he's doing here. I liked him straight off and I still like him, even though he's an oligarchist. We have the news on all day, a big screen by every row, silent but there. Having the wrath of the world on display nine hours a day gets us talking politics pretty often. I have to stop our conversations sometimes, when they start down a route I can see has no end.

The cleaner who takes care of my floor speaks only French. He's from the Ivory Coast and he plays the trombone. 'Côte d'Ivoire' sounds so smooth in the native accent. I'm the only French speaker still around when the cleaners come in. Either that or nobody else is interested. Anyway, we chat every day except Saturday – nobody cleans on a Saturday – and he must think my French is weak, because I can never think of anything new to say.

Sometimes it's nice to work a job you don't give a shit about. In the summer you don't have to worry about getting fired. Fun doesn't cost so much on a warm day. If you lose a job you can spend the days with your friends for a while – at least until you need money for food. Sometimes, if you've done alright, you can jack it in and get work when autumn starts showing. When the cold comes I find a job I like and try to stick at it till spring.

When the team next to us is busy I get left covering all our calls, because Simon and Pat both know the other team's work. It's a good thing really. They help us when we're about to go under and it's better for a business if everyone's flexible. Ian asks me to help them first, because he doesn't want my team's productivity to wane.

'I don't know how to do it,' I say.

'I thought I showed you,' he says.

Every day when I come in and say hi to him, he says he'll teach me the other accounts. I remind him of it later, when I'm not so busy, but he's never free.

'No,' I say, 'you were going to, but then you didn't.'

He's liking me less all the time.

I was making a round of coffee and I asked Ian, since his was black, if he wanted a dash of water on top. Ice and a slice, he said and a titter circulated. I don't ever want to be in a position where people have to laugh at my jokes.

All calls have to be logged into a warehouse circuit according to their urgency and stock type. I realised I'd entered a call into the wrong circuit and asked Ian to recall the job. Looking at it he asked why it was being dispatched from our depot.

'That's what we do for next day deliveries,' I said.

'No. There's no trunk on Saturdays,' he said. 'It has to go from the local depot.'

'Oh. We'd better take a look at the others I've done then.'

'Josh! I'm losing the will to live here.'

Don't stick around on my account, Ian. Still, it was a Saturday late shift and Ian ordered in a Chinese for us. No one took the piss, but we could more or less have whatever we wanted and it was understood that we keep it to ourselves. He'd brought in a bag of chocolate limes and passed them around earlier in the day and when the bag came back to him almost empty he made a joke of demanding repayment. We didn't have to wear a tie on Saturdays and nobody came in clean-shaven.

One evening the hospital called with an organ transit. Not wanting to cock it up, I asked Ian. He told me to take the details and he'd find a driver. I was to call them back. Ten minutes later they called again and I asked Ian 'Can we do it?' He said something like 'Well, I should think so, because we *are* a logistics company.' Sarcy cunt.

Daouda, the cleaner, invited me to go for a drink with him last week and on Saturday night, sitting in The Hillgrove, we found a conversation we could keep going. He wanted to know what sort of food I cooked. I said I could think of few things I didn't like. I told him about the Ngaus, who had taught me some Cantonese cooking, and he promised he'd teach me to make kedjenou, a chicken dish he said all Ivorians could cook. Daouda is a big man. It was nice to sit in a pub with such a big man.

Last Friday Ian told me off for talking to Daouda. I'd closed all the calls that were done so I went back to staring at my screen. Ian's rude to everyone, just sly little put-downs that alone aren't worth mentioning. But they add up. At the interview I thought him a miserable sod. He speaks in monotone. Hearing people talk like that reminds me of my old history teacher. Ian's lips looked all rubbery and I had the impression of saliva coating the area around his mouth.

After the first week I'd decided to like Ian. You could speak plainly with him and sometimes he made people laugh. I've since changed my mind again. Last week I answered the phone and it was for him.

'Ian, Lin from Certronics.'

'Okay, put her through.'

'What's your number again? Sorry, I've got a sieve for a memory.'

'You've got a sieve for fucking anything.'

He couldn't help it. He had to put me down.

When I was on my way out, Pat and Ian were still tidying up a few jobs. 'I'm off now, see you.'

'Yeah,' said Ian, 'see you next Tuesday.'

Daouda and I went picking for jam. I'd spied a few Mirabelle trees around Ridgeway Park and down Ardwell Lane. The plums were turning spotty and falling off the trees; some of them were squashed and rotting on the path. We should've had a net and shaken them off the trees, but we didn't have a net and anyway you can't use one with just two people. Instead we would give a gentle squeeze to test each one was ripe, twist it off and let it roll into the bowl from the edge. I ate some as we went; we both did. They were perfect, sweet and mellow. Juice flowed down my chin each time I broke the skin of a fresh one. We'd picked this one tree bare save the ones high up that only Daouda could reach. I took one from the floor and saw Daouda watch me. As I lifted it to my mouth he took it from me. 'C'est mauvais,' he said. It's bad. He pointed out the scar where the plum had split. He plucked another from the tree, felt it in his hand and dropped it behind him. He picked another and handed it to me.

At quarter to nine there were two calls left to close. Sunny had fitted a receipt printer at a Harvester in Wakefield. He sent the details on his Handy, without the serial number for the unit installed. I called him. Sorry, he said; he'd forgotten to take it down. I told him not to worry, I'd call them.

'Ian would've sent him back,' said Simon.

'And what a prick.'

Simon checked Ian was out of earshot. He took off his tie and put it in his drawer. 'I used to like him,' he said.

'Me too.'

'I'm not sure how much longer I'll last at this place.'

'Me neither.'

Then Ian told us to stop gassing. When I showed him what little work was left, he told me, 'Then it shouldn't take long.' Closing the jobs early wouldn't make a difference. We'd have to wait till ten to finish anyway, in case an emergency call came in and because we were on temporary contracts. Simon took the last one and phoned Rav. He had a parking ticket and said he didn't want to make deliveries to London anymore. Simon told him he'd have a word about getting the fine covered, but that not covering London would probably mean transferring to another branch. I knew, as did Simon, the company wouldn't cover any parking fines, but at least Rav could go home with a clear head.

Our team was called into the conference suite. Harry had cursed at someone while he thought one of our customers was on hold and a complaint was made to Ian's boss, whose name I don't even know.

Daouda walked around the office with a tray collecting mugs. Wherever someone who was still working had an empty mug at their desk he dithered. He knew how to ask if the mug was still wanted. The problem was that, not wishing to be rude, people generally answered in more than one word.

'Look, can you just fuck off. I'm trying to work,' I heard Ian say.

Daouda still dithered.

'Just fucking go. I'm busy.'

I got up and went over to Ian's desk. 'You need to learn how to talk to people,' I said.

'You what?'

'You can't talk to him like that. It does no good anyway; all he understands is that you're angry.'

'You need to mind your own fucking business. And your attitude.'

'Sod my attitude. You should know how to talk to people.'

Ian stood up and squared his shoulders with mine. 'You should know how to talk to your boss.'

'Yeah, because you stop being a person once you're a boss.'

'To you I do.'

I was about to reply when Daouda touched my shoulder. 'Attention,' he said, 'ton emploi.' I nodded. He was right; I wanted to stay. I looked back to Ian and told him I was sorry. He said we'd have a meeting the next day.

I came to work today with a letter of apology. Simon was late and there was plenty to process, so I got to work. Two hours into the shift Pat told me Simon had quit — temporary contract, no notice required. The team now consists of Pat and me, so Ian can't afford to lose either of us. I slid the letter into the paper bin.

Six-and-a-half Nights / *Keely O'Shaughnessy*

When Jack's sister, Emily, arrived unexpectedly at his flat, he knew immediately that her second marriage was over. She stayed a total of six-and-a-half nights, and every evening, after eating, they told each other ghost stories. On the fifth night, she asked him if he'd ever had an electric shock from having sex.

He had only ever had one real girlfriend — a blonde usherette he fumbled with at a re-screening of *Pet Cemetery*. She used to put her chewed gum into the popcorn warmer.

'Isn't it more static?' he asked.

'A zap that makes your hairs tingle.'

'Once, I think,' he said.

His sister frowned at him from her space on the sofa. She curled her stockinged toes over the edge of the seat and swayed to the radio, singing along: '*Here's big sister. We're big sister. Hear big sister. There's big sister. Dancing on your grave.*'

Jack sat on the floor beneath her and let the nylon of her tights rub against his skin.

'What are you doing here?' he said without looking up.

'Sitting?' she said.

Jack was ten years younger than Emily, and when she was sixteen, and boys would take her to marathons of Horror films at *Alexandra*, Jack would wait wrapped in his duvet and listen for her keys in the lock. A gentle sound like a scuffed shoe, and then the crackling air of a kiss. Jack would pretend to snore. He was happy the boys never came in. Sometimes his sister would press her lips over his eyelids and huddle with him on the stair, lifting his legs over hers. She would talk to him about the things she'd seen. Psychopaths and murders. She told him how David Bowie was a vampire and how arterial spray covered a back wall of a motel. That one was called *The Hunger*. Years later, Jack tried to steal a copy of the original film poster from the wall of a poetry café. The bartender had found him standing on a stool, tracing the gothic font with his finger.

Emily's room had been cake-frosting pink, the same colour as her tongue after candied shrimps. He used to watch in awe as she applied Blue Crackle nail varnish. 'Don't get it on you,' she'd say, 'it's acid!'

'It's magic, it's magic,' Jack would cry, too scared not to look.

She used to tell him they were playing a game. As innocent as hopscotch or cops and robbers. Jack would watch as she undressed. Tights rolled into doughnuts around her ankles, she would kick them off. Jack still remembered her naked body in the light of her flower-power lampshade. The triangles of her yet-to-develop breasts topped with gum drops and the spun sugar from the V between her legs.

'Stay still,' she had said, running a toy car the length of Jack's torso. His muscle car with over-sized wheels. It was orange and had Orlando written across the bonnet. The lampshade used to buzz. The current would sway and flicker as if generating life: the lightning bolts through Frankenstein's monster.

'I'm cutting you open now,' she said, digging him in the ribs so that he'd squirm. 'Don't struggle. You can't escape.'

The whirring of the windup mechanism was a bone saw. Jack arched his back and pushed his head into her pillow. The wheels churned up his skin leaving black sticky patches on his nipples. Sometimes Emily would drag the car too hard and Jack could hear the ticking over of it in his chest.

A pot of silly putty was his innards. Naked, she'd sit on his legs and role the slime between her hands into sausages. Jack could still remember the weight of her on his hips. She had a chicken pox scar just below her belly button.

'Most serial killers keep some sort of trophies from their victims,' she said. She spoke through her teeth like Hannibal Lector.

Now, she stood up, using Jack's collarbone as a springboard. 'Com'on, Jackie. Let's dance.' Winded, he watched as she turned the volume until the speakers rattled and then, wincing, he pulled himself up. It was a heavy metal song, but they danced a Jive. On the drawn out notes of the chorus his sister spun on the ball of her foot. Left and then right. *SisTER, sisTER, sisTER*. She twirled in to him. Jack mis-stepped on every beat. When the song finished the DJ announced that a freak show was coming to town and you could buy tickets by phoning a premium rate number. 'Book now to avoid disappointment,' said the DJ in a voice from the Big Top.

'We should go,' she said, relaxing into Jack's arms. The next song was a ballad about love. He thought about grains of sand draining through the neck of an egg timer. When she spoke again it matched the rhythm of the music.

'Jack? I need money.'

'Money?'

'Yes.'

'How much?'

'It's the house. I was chucked out.'

'What about Steve?' They spoke in whispers under the song on the radio.

'What about him? Why are you laughing?' she said. Jack stroked her hair, his fingers snagging the ends.

He thought about the boys she used to bring home to meet their mum, and the ones she didn't. Gary the Bartender who got the sack for drinking on the job or Spike the Goth turned drug dealer. Steve was the latest addition. He used to be her supervisor when she worked in the call centre. He wore a clip-on tie and kept a fountain pen in his shirt pocket that was still in the wrapper. Jack had been for a drink with him once. Steve had talked in a loud voice about the 'sweet bit of arse' that worked in the ordering department and how he wouldn't mind 'trotting out' a novel of his own.

'I haven't got any money,' Jack said. His laugh had become vibration. Open-mouthed. Movement, but no noise. He could see the fine down that covered her cheek.

'No, you're an academic.'

'I'm better than *any* of them, Em.'

Jack was pressed against the doughy flesh of his sister's upper-arm. He began to squirm but held her harder. His hand slid down the length of her thigh. The vibration stopped. The radio lost signal. Her breathing was as heavy as his. She lifted up her shirt. Jack made tiny noises, but didn't move away. Through the lace of her bra, she followed the circle of her honey-coloured nipples with her finger. He could feel his sister's other hand on his head, pushing him to her chest. He rested his lips against her nipple, neither consenting nor resisting. But when she jerked her body, he lifted himself off and slumped on to her shoulder. The undrawn window had become a mirror that reflected their silhouettes; the only light was the glow from the stereo's digital panel. He had gone limp.

'Fuck,' he sobbed.

'Don't be an asshole.' Her voice splintered off… 'I haven't got anyone else.' Emily stood rubbing her breast with her palm. He expected her to say something, but she didn't. Jack saw that her nails were ridged and unpainted. He sniffed back tears and then tried to kiss her neck. She turned her head away and started re-clipping the buttons of her shirt. They sat side by side, shoulders touching, eyes fixed straight ahead.

Later, standing hunched over the washbasin in the bathroom, Jack let his eyes adjust to the glare of the strip light. The sink was lined with long hairs, some trying to escape the rim. Against the white they seemed more copper than blonde. Jack washed his face and then sluiced the bowl, watching as the hairs drained away. Outside he could hear Emily had started the washing up. There was the clank of cutlery. The bathroom had been invaded by her toiletries. They lurked together in packs: oversized shampoo and conditioner bottles that dribbled slime from their plungers; a witch-hazel face scrub, half of its label obscured by the purple of a lavender Radox. The side where he kept his razor had been captured too; nail varnishes queued like a Dulux colour chart, and these were mingled with pots of cream, nail varnish remover, clippers and files that looked like implements of torture. Stepping back, Jack took a swipe. This was in slow motion. The mechanical spring of a pinball flipper. With a dragnet movement of his arm, along the length of the surface, he scattered the collection of bottles on to the floor. After the clatter, a lone sideways varnish spilled its contents off the edge of the sideboard. A neon waterfall. The smell was toxic. Hands clamped to his nose and mouth, Jack sank to his knees. Around him colours marbled together and rippled like spilled petrol.

Jack didn't want to stay in the house with Emily, and so, at just gone ten, he put a plaster on his bleeding hand and walked. He had passed The Westfield every day for years, but had never before gone in. The young barmaid wore pink lipstick and didn't seem to notice the multicoloured hand smears that covered his jeans. He found a seat in an armchair far away from people, but close enough to see the TV above the bar. The woman on Sky News shuffled her papers and patted her hair. Sitting down, Jack opened the crisp packet along the seam and spread it flat on the table. The news had switched from the studio to what looked like a hospital. The subheading read Manchester's St Mary's Hospital. There was no sound. The reporter stood in the waiting area gesturing with too much emotion. The story was about the separation of conjoined twins. The subtitles said that they had been given the pseudonyms Mary and Jodie to protect their identity. If they were separated the doctors knew Mary would die. Jack sipped his drink and watched as the screen projected images of a Catholic priest. The reporter was asking whether murder is more a moral or religious concern. In the bar, people cheered as pool balls were potted. The barmaid wiped down a table ready for a family. She clicked chewing gum with her tongue.

Jack thought about Emily. If you heated skin you could easily weld two bodies together. Flesh knitting to flesh like a healing scab. The TV now showed examples of the medical equipment the doctors would have to use. There were what looked like massive pinking-shears and two pairs of forceps. Jack wondered what life would be like fused to another human. Feeling an irreplaceable closeness. He imagined bathing side by side, water magnifying the scar. How good it would be to know someone else's body as well as your own. The best place to be joined, Jack decided, would be the arm; that way they could be plated together. Jack stroked his forearm with his right hand. He imagined Emily damp with saline solution. Thick interweaved stitches like rope pulling the skin taut. An overstretched balloon. He would wash it every day making sure the swelling was going. They would need a new name. The term used to describe a dependant twin is 'parasitic.' The subtitles said that the medical team had realised that Mary's heart and lungs were so poorly developed that she was totally dependent on Jodie for oxygen and blood circulation. She (Mary) could not exist without Jodie.

The family to Jack's right had started reading the snack menu to their children. The boy shuffled a deck of cards and the girl blew bubbles into her cola. The mum asked about chicken nuggets and the boy laid six cards face down in front of his sister. He asked her to pick one. She blew harder into the glass until the froth rose to the top. When she didn't point the boy picked a card himself and placed it back in the pack without looking. The magic came from the black box that held the cards. Jack used to have one when he was little. It came with magician's rings and a wand. A hidden compartment in the box slid back when the drawer was opened so it looked as if the chosen card had vanished. The boy showed the girl the card was missing. Angry and confused that her brother was capable of such power, she knocked her drink into her lap. The sugary liquid seeped through her Hello Kitty T-shirt. As the girl began to sob, the boy didn't laugh like Jack expected; instead, he unrolled a napkin from his cutlery and attempted to mop up the mess.

The Sky News logo flashed after an ad break. A diagram of the twins explained the medical facts. The sisters were joined at the lower abdomen but they were able to lie flat on their backs. At first glance they appeared as if they were one single trunk with a head and limbs at both ends. The picture was labelled and numbered with lines and arrows. Although their spines were fused, their legs were independently formed and criss-crossed each other. The programme had not given the baby any features – just a 2D stencil. Jack thought about the surviving baby's return to Malta. A small village with cobble-stoned streets lined with people waving banners. 'Congratulations'?

When he returned home, Jack noticed the cushions had been plumped and the remotes placed in their holders. In the bathroom everything had been tidied away. A large pink vanity case with a sponge pushed through the carry-handle on the sideboard, and Jack's wash bag had been placed in the soap dish next to the hot tap. The only sign of the incident was a small patch of colour that spread across the tiles like a faint birthmark. The stain was most pronounced in the grouting where the varnish had pooled in the gullies between each square.

Emily was asleep in his bed like an embryo. She was foetal with a pillow between her thighs. When he got in beside her she didn't stir. Her breath was so slight Jack thought about checking her pulse. Her veins were raised like braille.

'Are you awake?' he whispered.

And I Feel Fine / *Matthew Benson*

The first thing Simon noticed was the brightness of the room. The second was the smell, like kitchen tiles. There were already three people there so he bolted the door. His earphones sat snug, crackling and distorting the song. *This one goes out to the one I love.* He was carrying a rucksack on his back and a large framed picture under his left arm. *This one goes out to the one I left behind.* The rucksack had two changes of clothes, a laptop, a sixteen-part Swiss Army knife, three books and some basic ration packs in case they were in there longer than expected. That was what he had been told to bring. *A simple prop, to occupy my time.* He was also carrying his MP3 player, a clarinet in a travel case, seven unfinished music manuscripts, a bottle of forty-year-old whisky, and ten Cuban cigars, which he promised himself he would smoke before he died. He pulled out his earphones.

'I'm glad you made it,' Karen said.

'I thought it was only going to be the three of us.' Simon shook hands with Lee, Karen's husband, who had been sitting in the corner with a woman Simon didn't know. 'Hi Lee.'

'Yeah, I didn't have time to let you know. That's my sister, Laura. She was meant to go,' Karen told him. 'Her husband decided to take his mistress instead, though.'

'Nice guy.'

Karen dropped her voice. 'She can't have kids. Her husband made some excuse about saving someone who could help the human race. He's wanted to divorce her for ages, but hasn't had the balls.' Karen rubbed the corners of her eyes with her index finger and thumb. 'She's tough. Don't feel sorry for her.' She pointed to the corner, next to her sister. 'Your bed's that one over there.'

The single bed was light canvas in a metal frame, and the blanket and pillow were thin, easy to move. There was also a small table for his things, against which leaned a folding plastic chair. He rested the picture on the desk, against the wall, then dropped his rucksack on the bed and opened it. He put his laptop on the table, then pulled the clothes out of the bag and put them in the drawer under the bed. Kicking the rucksack under the table, he decided to have a look around the shelter. The most interesting thing was at the very back: a small room, holding the toilet and shower. It smelled offensively clean, like someone trying to cover the smell of citrus with the smell of honey with the smell of lavender. There was a drone coming from behind the wall: probably a water purifier for the tanks under the shelter. Most of the purifiers he had seen for sale had been huge things that required a lot of power and produced even more noise. This machine was probably expensive, but solar powered and quiet. Sometimes having moneyed-up neighbours wasn't so bad.

He was back in his corner within five minutes of leaving. Picking up the picture he'd brought, he sat on the bed. Some people considered the picture distasteful, others called it disrespectful. A man holding a gun, pointed at another man's head. Two people in the close background, one far off. Black and white. In the foreground, one man has just pulled the trigger.

'Hi, I'm Laura.'

Simon turned to look at her. 'Oh, hi. Simon.' He noticed her eyes were still puffy, but dry now. She wore pearls like anyone else would wear a jacket.

'Nice to meet you.' They shook hands.

Simon propped his pillow against the wall and leant on it, but he could still feel the wall. 'So.' He coughed.

'Why do we have to be down here, do you think? I mean, nothing's going to happen.' She was looking at the picture while talking.

'What do you mean?'

'Well, they didn't even tell us anything, did they?'

'They didn't want to panic anyone.' He noticed the way she spoke, and it didn't match the rest of her.

'It's just weird. I mean, I want to know what's happening.' Laura sat down on the chair. 'You bring this with you?' She nodded her head at the picture. 'It's kind of creepy.'

'I think it's amazing.'

The men were framed by trees to the left and buildings to the right. The road and the sky tapered off before you could see them join.

'How so?'

'It tells us who we are. It tells us everything wrong with ourselves. Not just what's happening in it, but–' He rubbed the stubble he was trying to grow into a beard. 'Do you think it's disgusting?'

'Yeah. Well… kind of. It's just… creepy.'

'Exactly. This guy, Nguyen Van Lem, is stuck halfway between life and death. The picture was taken in 1968. He's been dying since then. People are so fascinated by what it means that they can't form an opinion. It's just–' He put the picture against the wall, facing out, and moved his hands behind his head. 'Epic.'

'It's creepy. 1968?'

'Yeah, he was a Vietcong operative. The guy shooting him is called Nguyen Ngoc Loan, I think.' Simon rubbed his hand over the picture, clearing a few specks of dust from the frame.

'I can't believe he's just shooting the guy in the head like that.'

'Van Lem wasn't a good guy. He was a murderer. He killed Ngoc Loan's family.'

'Oh.' Laura was thinking.

'It's not black and white.'

'Yes it is.'

'What?'

'The photo, it's black and white.'

'I meant the event.'

'Oh.' Laura was leaning forward, staring at Van Lem's expression. 'It's strange. It looks like he's been punched.'

Simon nodded. Van Lem's expression wasn't pain, it was discomfort. Simon had read an article about the photo. It said that on the high quality ones you could see the bullet exiting his head. But he'd paid a lot of money for the photo to be blown up to the size it was, and he couldn't afford the extra to make it the same definition as the small photo. He wished he could see the bullet because when he'd found that out he'd felt like the photo didn't work anymore. There was something missing. Not like a jigsaw with a lost piece, more like a car without oil.

'I'm going to have something to eat, I think.' She stood up and started walking away from Simon. 'Do you want anything?'

'No thanks. I don't feel like eating. I might listen to some music.' He paused, but didn't move.

Laura nodded, and then walked back to her bed.

He put his headphones in and pressed play.

Sometime later, Simon felt someone shake him. He made a noise, but didn't open his eyes. He wasn't sure if he'd been asleep. The others had been talking. They might have just finished, and Simon might have missed everything. He opened his eyes, and then half-closed them. It was bright in the shelter, like the sun reflecting off a wet road. He stopped the music.

'Simon, wake up.' It was Karen.

'I'm awake.'

'You scared my sister.' She took a deep breath, like she was about to shout. Simon looked at her. 'You… with your picture… thing!'

'What do you mean?'

'You filled her head with all this stuff about people killing people. Isn't this bad enough?' She swept her arm backwards, towards the door.

'She asked me about it.'

'You didn't have to tell her.'

'She *asked* me. Why are you treating her like a kid?'

'I'm not treating her like a kid. You could have just given her the facts!'

'I did!'

'Well, then, you should have said it wasn't important.' She folded her arms. It made her look like a teacher.

'But it is important.'

Karen looked like she was thinking, the same way she would if she'd been put in check. 'What gives you the right to decide what's important?' She spoke like a child reading something they hadn't seen before.

Simon picked at the top of his teeth with his tongue before speaking. 'We're the last. Whatever we have, that's society, culture, now. We remember bad things, but this is proof. More people care about war after seeing this than after a dozen Remembrance Day celebrations.' This wasn't the reason Simon loved the picture. He couldn't say why he loved it. The last time he tried he'd sounded psychotic.

'It's distasteful.'

'D'you have a problem with violent films?' Simon was being rhetorical, but Karen shook her head.

'That's what I thought. This is no different.'

'It's different, Simon, because this is real.'

'The man in the photo would be dead by now anyway. You don't know him. Hell, there's been worse stuff than this in documentaries.'

'Look.' She spoke like she'd changed her mind after the first word. 'Keep it. You're not a bad person. Just... Turn it around. You don't have to get rid of it. We'll be here a few days at most. Death is just the last thing we want to think about.'

'OK.' He picked the picture up and looked at it again before turning it and resting it on the desk against the wall. 'I'm sorry. I get caught up by it.'

'We're not saying it's not interesting, Simon. It's just, now, with all this...' She pointed at the door again. Simon couldn't tell if she was pointing at it on purpose. 'I'm sorry. I don't mean to keep going on about it.' She smiled at him, but walked away before he could speak. He started biting his nails and remembered when he was younger, getting the 'not angry, disappointed' speech. He still had his headphones in so he pressed play.

Sitting on his bed with his back to the wall, eyes half closed, headphones in, Simon could see the others talking. The bed smelled mostly of old clothes, things stored at the bottom of a chest of drawers for years, but there was something faint that was bothering him, almost like cumin. Laura was crying – again – and Lee was walking towards him. After a moment of thought, Simon decided he couldn't ignore him. He pulled his headphones out and slid to the edge of the bed.

The chorus of the song was playing, but he couldn't make it out; it was just a faint buzzing. He paused it.

'What you listening to?' Lee said.

'R.E.M.'

'Cool.' He sat next to Simon. It seemed almost fatherly, uncomfortable, like he was about to give 'the talk.'

'The picture—'

'Yeah, Karen and I spoke about that. Sorry if it freaked you out.'

'It's not me.'

'No, really, I'm sorry. I just get kind of... caught up, you know?' Simon stood and ran his palm along the edge of the frame.

'I thought you were going to get rid of it.'

'What?'

'Karen, she wants it gone.'

'She said she was OK with it just turned around.'

'They're kind of scared.'

'What do you want me to do about it, Lee?'

'Get rid of it.'

'I can't.'

'Why not?'

'Because. It's important.'

'What the hell is wrong with you, Simon?'

'Sorry?'

Lee stood up as well. He was taller than Simon by a good six inches. Simon was expecting something like in films, where they squared up to each other, staring, when there's too much hate for words. Simon didn't want to step forward. Lee didn't move.

'Get rid of it.'

'No.'

'Then get out.'

'What?'

'Get out.' Lee whispered, but Karen and Laura both turned to look at them.

'Don't be ridiculous.'

'Throw the picture out.'

'You're overreacting.'

'Throw it, or get out.' Lee seemed to move forward without moving his feet. 'In fact, just get out. Find somewhere else.'

'What are you going to do, Lee? You want your wife to see this?'

Lee moved forward and walked past Simon. Karen had her arm around Laura's shoulder. Neither of them said anything, though Karen looked like she wanted to. Simon was sure he could hear his heart beating. Lee opened a drawer in the kitchen and shuffled cutlery back and forward, like he was looking for something. It sounded like he was pouring coins onto a desk. He pulled out a knife.

'You going to stab me, Lee?'

'If I need to, yes.'

'You've lost it, man.'

'Get out, then.'

Simon didn't reply. Instead, he picked up the rucksack and pushed his laptop into it, then grabbed the clothes from the drawer under his bed and forced them in on top of everything. When he put the bag on his back it felt heavier than before. He put his headphones in, then picked up the picture and put it under his arm. He didn't look at any of them as he walked to the door. Or as he opened it. He hit play. *See you in heaven if you make the list*. As he walked out, he thought he heard Lee say something. It probably wasn't worth listening to.

Ripening / *Rose Fowler*

The mirror in the girls' toilets is smeared with lipstick and waxy fingerprints. The toilet in our school is partly underground, so the window is long and narrow, high up against the ceiling, with a wide windowsill. It is possible to sit up there if you take a running jump from by the door. I watch the other girls preening. These girls are my friends. If I narrow my eyes enough they all look the same. The air is clogged with hairspray, but up by the ceiling it's a little easier to breathe. The walls are painted bright yellow, and with the strip lights and metal basins the room gives an impression of stoic cheerfulness. The window is murky plastic and crossed with grid lines like the sheets of paper we get in maths. Outside I can see the tennis courts and the legs of passing students. School has its own government, its own set of laws. One of the laws here is that to avoid persecution all girls must wear skirts, and there's no such thing as too short. (The boys get shouted at for undoing their top buttons or loosening their ties, but the teachers don't say a thing about our skirts). This may be a patriarchal society, but this law has been laid down by the girls.

The chatter ceases as the door opens and Betty Jones walks in. Betty is a fat girl's name. I wonder what her parents were thinking. Betty isn't really fat, but she's got the biggest boobs in our year and what my mum calls a 'generous behind,' which is the reason no one's allowed to talk to her. I feel sorry for her. The silence follows her out the door.

'God, what a whale,' I say.

My sister doesn't need to tell me that she's jealous of my body. She said that when I get to her age I will swell like fruit, like all the women in our family. I think of overripe plums, the unpleasant way they burst when you bite into them, collapsing inwards as juice spurts out, flesh brownish at the centre. I think of the pendulous movement of milk-heavy breasts and my trunk and thighs thickening, growing sturdy and full. I've started eating only at night. As soon as everyone else is asleep I go downstairs and gorge myself on fatty chicken skin and doughnuts, pizza and cookies and bowls of cereal, eating until my stomach hurts and bulges out. I wake every morning feeling packed and guilty and I vow not to eat for as long as I can.

'I don't know. I wouldn't mind having her tits,' says Georgia.

'Oh, fuck off. You'd need plastic bags to carry them in. Like, not to be harsh or anything, but she doesn't exactly try to hide them, does she? I mean, come on. Get that out of my face,' Kelly replies.

'She's just a slag. If she can't even respect herself, how does she expect anyone else to?' Jen looks up from her lip gloss, catching everyone's eyes in the mirror, challenging anyone to speak.

'I had to sit by her in music once. She's actually pretty nice,' says Sophie, the only non-blonde in the group.

'You actually talked to her?' Jen rounds on her. Jen's shoes have tiny kitten heels, exaggerating the slim muscles in her calves.

'Only once. I mean, I wasn't interested, she just wouldn't stop trying to get my attention.'

'Whatever.' Jen turns back to the mirror, sucking in her cheeks and moving her head to study different angles of her face.

I was late to school this morning, again. I woke at five but lay motionless, facing the wall for what must have been hours, until I saw the wedge of light widen and felt the soft thump of weight on my bed. I felt a hand on my shoulder and though Mum's voice was gentle her fingers were gripping my skin to the point of pain.

'When did you last eat?'

We're not allowed inside at lunchtime, even in winter, and there's only so much time you can spend in a toilet. Traipsing out into the cold, we huddle in a circle in our usual corner of the tennis courts, heads bent against the wind. The other girls pull out lunchboxes and I watch, repelled, as they bite into spongy sandwiches and chocolate bars, tearing open packets of crisps. The mingling smells are heady. My jaw aches and there's a stale, metallic taste in my mouth.

'Ooouuuch. What happened to you?' I follow Georgia's gaze to my knuckles. They've swollen up since last night.

'Oh,' I shrug, 'that prick Rick Wooders slammed my hand in a door.' Georgia's face stretches into an exaggerated expression of shock.

'No! He didn't.'

I look over at Jen. Her folded legs are the shape of swans' necks. She's not eating either.

Actually, he didn't, but I don't say this. Rick Wooders is okay; he's just more sad than most people, so he shouts louder. What really happened was that my dad came home drunk last night (isn't that how all interesting stories start? Nothing good comes out of a story beginning with the father waking up well-rested, or eating a salad). I could hear him yodelling and cursing from all the way down the street. My parents don't fight. They don't talk at all.

When he came in (six seconds of the key scratching around the lock) I didn't hear anything for a long time, but I still couldn't sleep. I padded downstairs to peer around the doorjamb. My father was sitting in the kitchen, his back to me, eating a long-cold dinner, a single candle lit before him, no music playing. That was unusual. Dad never eats without a musical accompaniment. For dinner it's usually Dvorák, Rimsky-Korsakov or Sibelius. (For some reason, during these port-sodden evenings he becomes obsessed with European Romantic composers, specifically those influenced by folk music from their own countries. He has never been to any of these countries, nor has he any family connection, but during the second movement of Smetana's Má Vlast, he always stands, grim and proud like an ancient war hero.) My mother cleaned as she moved around him. Neither acknowledged the other's presence. I went into the sitting room and perched in the middle of the sofa, waiting. There is a clock in our sitting room on the mantelpiece over the fireplace. It is small and squat, made of shiny wood and fake gold, with a large face. I watched the hands ticking around. Nothing happened. Eventually I stood up and I hit the clock with my fist as hard as I could. Its face cracked and it fell to the ground. I stood still, holding my hand and my breath, but still nothing happened.

That was a lie. I don't know my father at all. He left us when I was little.

Jen takes a small plastic bag out of her handbag with a small white stick inside. Looking up she sees me staring before I can look away, and jerks her head back towards the playing field and stands up. Any other day I'd probably hang my head and wait for the bell to ring, but today feels different. Go with the flow, right? I scramble to my feet and tentatively follow her.

When my mother gripped my shoulder, my face scrunched and convulsed like that of an ugly baby, though few actual tears came. It wasn't guilt about eating, so much as guilt about gorging on my Mum's supplies, hard-earned from long hours in the harsh lights of the pharmacy. I rolled myself up, knees to chest, facing away from her concern and prying. I felt I had to hold my skeleton together or the bones would fly apart, coated in greasy ash and rags of skin. I didn't want to admit what I'd done, but otherwise she'd find out herself. She wouldn't say anything, but she would know and I would know and I don't think I could stand that. So I told her about my feeding frenzy.

'Slow down, honey. What do you mean you ate all the brownies? We don't have any brownies.'

I didn't understand. I could still feel the shiny skin of the brownies giving way into dense chocolate under my teeth.

The grass is soaking and, after a while, so are my feet, but I don't complain as we return to the back fence, the furthest we can get from the school. The ground here is littered with cigarette butts, empty beer cans, Monster Munch packets, broken glass and even a used condom. Jen lights up with one of those coloured Poundland lighters that look like lollipops. We make seats out of our bags, and she passes me the joint. I breathe the acrid stuff into my mouth and choke, coughing out smoke, my throat raw.

Jen laughs. 'Not like that, dumbass. Haven't you ever smoked before? Try again. Breathe. Hold it in your mouth. Now, in again, down to the bottom of your chest.'

I try again and manage it properly this time, then toke again greedily, pulling the smoke in deep and slow, dizziness washing over me.

'That's it. Hey, quit hogging,' Jen says. I hand it back.

'Wow,' she laughs at me, 'you really haven't ever done this before. Look at your face, man.' I press my fingers to my face. It feels like cold pig flesh. Jen shakes her head. I lean back, enjoying the coolness of the wet grass on my head and the aching stretch in my lower back. The clouds are the colour of wet slate but the light is heavy, sick yellow: a doomsday sky.

After some time – hard to say exactly how long – in silence, passing the joint back and forth, Jen speaks again.

'I can't be fucked to go back,' she says, looking across to the cluster of grey school buildings. 'Want to ditch?' I haven't skived before. Not properly. I once hid in the toilet for an hour to get out of P.E. and pretended I'd got stuck in the cubicle, but no one believed me and I got into loads of trouble. I was so ashamed I haven't tried it since.

I can't face my mother's questions, her bright post-it notes stuck around the kitchen with scrawled reminders to herself, the big diet plan she's stuck to the fridge, her over-cheerful face.

'Yeah, okay,' I say.

'Sweetheart. You know we don't have any chocolate in the house. You know your sister is lactose intolerant, don't you?' Her voice was now tinged with something else under the façade of calm. Of course, I remembered. Of course we can't have any chocolate. Bex is so allergic we just don't bother buying any.

'No, no.' I was insisting. I vividly remembered rows of double chocolate muffins in the cupboard under the sink, the heaps of dolly mix on the shelves in the pantry, the cheeseburgers layered in the fridge, no time to warm them, gulped down cold; the plasticky cheese and meat was thick and gluey and hard to chew. Mum looked at me oddly and I felt bizarre panic. My stomach was hard, hot, bulging. I can't be crazy. It happened. It *happened*.

Calling it hunger doesn't do it justice. It's an addiction. I can barely fight my body. I am a hero, a champion. I am powerful. No one else can do what I can do. There are chip shops and burger joints and noodle stands and fruit stalls and my mouth waters as I watch people devouring this mass of fat and calories, all this food they don't need, and they are weak where I am strong.

Jen gets alcohol, I don't know how. Everything is blurry and hard to keep focused. There is a smallish bottle of Glenn's vodka, but I don't need much. We drink it straight on the streets, giggling and using our bodies to hide each other as we swig. The taste burns my throat and makes me gag but after a while I can't taste it anymore. The hunger is still there, but disconnected, unimportant. The world is growing colder and darker.

'Where shall we go?'

'Dunno. There's nowhere *to* go. '

'Then let's go nowhere! C'mon.'

Jen's hand in mine. I lock our fingers. She pulls me into a run, switching down streets and alleys at random. It is all just a game.

It's hard to keep my eyes open when I am so sleepy. Only Jen's jerks at my arm keep me from falling. Then there are lights. Thousands of coloured lights.

'In here!' I cry. 'Look at these *lights*! They're amazing!'

'Yeah, well, so's your face!' This is hilarious. We stagger about, blind from laughter.

When I think of funfairs I'm reminded of childhood and summer, heat-withered grass and the back of my mother's knees as she led me around by my hand, which was always sticky from candyfloss. But these memories don't add up with the black, icy air of tonight, the taste of vodka and my breath puffing out white. The lights swirl, garish in the dark. We're laughing and slipping on the wet grass and leaf mulch. Jen's face is suddenly close to mine. Her lips are the unnatural colour of berries. I've never kissed anyone before, but my mouth seems to know what to do. She doesn't resist and I think, okay, it's okay, it's just the vodka. I want to kiss her harder, fiercely, bite her lip, tear into her, rip her apart with my teeth. We are on a Ferris wheel, and the heights and movement make my vision flare and sway. I grip the rail, concentrating on how ice-cold it is, concentrating on not throwing up.

'Hey, Jen?'

'Yeeeeeaaah.'

'Do you ever, like. I dunno, feel like hey. Is this it? Is this everything there is? I mean, really?'

'Dude, that sounds so cheesy.'

'But. There's all this *stuff*, right, and I just think, what's the point? Don't you ever get sad?'

'Everyone gets sad sometimes.'

'I mean really sad.' Jen looks at me and for a moment every boundary has vanished. I get this sense that she understands me entirely. She smiles in a hard way.

'That's why we drink and smoke,' she says. 'You, my dear, need a fag. Let's get off this thing.'

We are on the ground again, but the ground is moving more than the Ferris wheel.

'I'm so drunk,' I keep saying, 'I'm SOOO drunk!'

Jen is talking to a boy. This boy seems to have a friend and his friend is talking to me, but I have no idea what the friend is saying so I just nod and smile and try not to fall over and then the friend is gone but he's back holding something white and square and big and holding it out to me and—

Her fingers closed around my wrist and it burned. I yanked my arm away and vaulted over her in a sudden burst of energy, slamming myself into the bathroom before she could even react. Sliding the lock into the catch I faded out her voice on the other side, quiet and reasonable but with that distinguishable high note of fear. I put one foot up on the side of the bath, and, holding the shower rail, got the other foot up and turned myself around to face the mirrored doors of the cabinet over the sink. Awkwardly, with one hand, I pulled my T-shirt off, clinging onto the rail with my other hand. There was a flash of something ugly. Hipbones and ribs in staccato ridges, skin like cling film, a greyish pallor. And then it was gone. The heat and the hardness remained. I turned to the side, examining the D my stomach made, rubbing my hand over the taut, rounded bulk. Like a pregnancy, I thought. I'm pregnant with food.

It's a box of chips. Oh God I can smell them, feel the heat from them, smell that greasy salty smell, and they are golden and squashy and Jen takes one and if Jen can have one why can't I? I try to count up how many calories would be in just a single chip let alone this whole pile but I can't focus and I'm SO HUNGRY GODDAMN IT I AM SO FUCKING HUNGRY YOU HAVE NO IDEA. I take a chip. It burns my tongue but I gulp it down regardless and then I lose control – I am at the mercy of my body and I'm grabbing them by the handful, shoving them into my mouth, my hands slick, my lips burning from salt. I can see their eyes on me but it feels so fucking good, even though I can barely taste them now and my jaw is aching and I am so ashamed, so ashamed at their expressions but I cannot stop until there are no chips left and there are only looks of horror, and 'Oh my God what the fuck? What a *freak*' and worse, *laughter*, and I can feel my stomach, huge and painful, and I need to get away from this so I turn and try to run but I can only waddle and I get to some toilets – festival portaloos – and I clamber in and lock the door. It's dim and foul in here but nothing matters except this massive panic swelling up, crushing my lungs.

I ram my fingers down my throat, twisting them until a splatter of vodka hits the pan. The chips are stodgy and I choke them up in small lumps. Mucus hangs in two thick ropes from my mouth and nose, dangling into the bowl. I retch, again and again, tasting the rank mix of salt and alcohol as the chips come back up. The toilet is full of sludge and nothing more is coming, but my stomach is cramping violently and I can't stop spitting yellowish saliva. The fear is receding. At last I ease my spine back into alignment and lift my T-shirt, touching shaking fingers to my stomach. There is no D here, but a cave. There are xylophone ribs poking out of my skin. I am perfect. I peer into the smudgy mirror. Bile and snot and drool cover my hand and lower face. My cheeks have streamed black, and little purple cracks have appeared under my eyes from burst blood vessels. The corners of my mouth are red and swollen. I look like a Joker clown. It is too painful to swallow. My mouth tastes like rot. I am a monster.

Stumbling back into the cold air I find that the purge has sobered me. The funfair is an insane pile of bright colours and thudding music off to my right. I walk the opposite way, and finally flop down in the dark, wet grass. The night sky is clear, the view only slightly marred by the red haze in the sky behind me. I don't move for a long time. My limbs become numb. I wonder vaguely what happened to Jen. What she thought of me. I can't face going to school tomorrow, but tomorrow is a long way off. The idea of a future past tonight is unbearable. In a minute I might go home, to my mum. To be cradled in her arms while I cry. I'll ask her if she'll bring me tea and stay with me until I fall asleep. I'll tell her everything. I swear. I don't want this anymore, not any of it. I'll ask her why Dad left. I will. In a minute.

Sex Education / *Katie Farmer*

When I was nine I watched a BBC documentary about African elephants. Mum was upstairs reading Derek his favourite story – a Goldilocks style rip-off called 'That's Not My Spoon' – while I watched a baby elephant wrapping its trunk around a hidden camera.

The picture rattled up and down before giving us a five second close-up of a square of sand broken apart with pebbles and sprigs of green, and then the ground rolled up into the sky.

'It is extraordinary. A calf's eye view has never been seen before on TV,' the voiceover said. 'Meanwhile, Shila has separated from the rest of the herd. She is in heat and must attract a mate or wait another year.'[1] A shot of Shila wandering alongside a shrub I now know to be an acacia. 'She's in luck. A male has caught her scent.'

Shila paused, watched the male swagger towards her, and then turned and ran. He jolted forwards, trunk stiff, ears splayed out. Elephants are all knees when they run. They hold their heads up to keep themselves steady but their legs shake with the weight.

'Cows can normally outrun the male. Shila, however, has not yet recovered from her clash with the poachers.'

There was a metre-long vacuum hose between his legs. A fucking *vacuum* hose. It waggled as the elephant ran. To the right, to the left, in circles, its blunt end flicking up and down.

I shuffled into a sitting position and stared at the open door. From my seat I could see the curved overhang of the first step. I scurried into the landing. A slit of light from Derek's door rested on Granddad's painting of a phone box.

'"No," sighed the big brown bear. "That's not my spoon. My spoon had three Bs on the handle. Oh, what am I to do?"'

They'd have been two thirds of the way through. In ten minutes she'd send him to wash his face while she heated up a goodnight 'milky-moo' in the microwave.

'The male rests his trunk on Shila's flank.'

He slung it right around so the snout grazed her back. His mouth was open into a Disney smile, all turned up at the corners like Dumbo, and his bottom lip rubbed her below the backbone.[2]

That night, I lay curled up to the left of the bed, my forehead pressing into

---

1 I wouldn't know what 'in heat' meant until year five when the teachers sent the boys to watch *Blackadder* with Ms Alders the history teacher. I spent the hour scratching pink fluff off the carpet while a French woman showed us how much a tampon could swell in a glass of water.

2 I saw this movie when my parents left me at Uncle Simon's for a week while they bonded with Derek in Pembrokeshire. It kept me awake longer than the heffalumps in Winnie the Pooh.

my bedside table. I counted all of my characters and thought of my fox pirate, Bloodeyes, and his lioness wife, Leopatre, and their two cubs.

Derek mewed in the next room, crawling out of bed and pawing his way to our parents' door. He'd sleep like that until he was seven and the new dog ousted him from his position in-between my parents.

I carried this feeling of knowing into school and sat it down between Dami and Daisy as they argued about whether I should play football or Stuck in the Mud. I told them I'd decide before the disco and wandered off to the library. They didn't understand and the librarian couldn't answer my questions so I took my knowledge home and hoped my Mum would answer the door. She didn't.

'Look. Noony people in net.' Derek had been in his spaceship – a five-foot long cardboard box with BEDROOM scrawled across the lid. He kept his crew in there – a selection of thirty toys that travelled with him and fought monsters. He'd wedged a pole from his Spiderman play-set into the corner of his ship and hung a net from the end. Between the gaps, my old Barbies beamed up at me, their legs and arms knotted around each other.

'Why'd you do that, Derek?'

'I didn't.'

'Who did?'

'Derek Club With Spikes On His Club.'[3]

'Are they gonna escape?'

'Buzz and the Action Men will save them.'

Buzz Lightyear and four trouser-less Action Men lay in a semi-circle below. Motorbike Man had his fist pointing at his kidnapped girlfriend.

'Kitgirl could kick her way out.' I reached down and flipped the leg that wasn't held on by tape.

'No.'

Derek had discovered and renamed my dolls after the move. Rose, the athletic bitch, became Flowergirl. She married Buzz and had six little Buzzes. Belle the horse rider became Kitgirl – a cavewoman prone to epileptic fits and bouts of cartoon violence. He stole three others – the poppy twins and my mermaid – but they did fuck all. He'd opened them up and jammed them back together and now Kitgirl was lacking a neck and half of her left leg.

'Where's Mum?' I was staring out the window. Maybe I was looking at my rabbits picking at the grass or maybe they'd died by then and I was staring at the scuffs on the patio where their hutch used to be.[4]

'Uglebug.'

---

3   The villain of Derek's stories. He believed all bad guys should have a signature weapon. He stole his from his favourite Spyro Boss. Apparently, mine was a sword. With daggers on.
4   The patio ended up being where my Mum did all her gardening. She'd tried planting tulips and orchids but they never sprouted. She put it down to the 'no-good Belgian soil.' It was swamp soil. The only things that grew in it were weeds and maggots.

'That's not a word.'

'It is. It is. It is.'

'Not.'

'People say it.' He slammed Buzz into the net. The Barbies shuddered and fell onto their boyfriends.

Maybe it was a word. Maybe it was Dutch. I never learnt Dutch. They only taught French at The British Primary and The BSB but every kid down my road was Flemish. According to a letter addressed to a Mr C Fitzgerald, I lived in Sint-Stevens-Woluwe in the municipality of Zaventem. Our landlord, Henri, had built the house on a hill opposite a football pitch. He lived in the house next to ours and kept chickens in the vegetable pen and an ex-police dog in a cage at the back of his garden.[5] He expected my parents to be mid-fifties and have grandchildren that visited at Christmas and Easter. He expected them to drink lager and invite him to dinner parties where he would mingle with the folks at NATO. Instead, he and his wife, Marguerite, spent their free time babysitting Derek and me.[6]

Derek shoved his toys off his lap and stood up. His trousers remained in the spaceship with his Action Men.

'Derek. Put some pants on.'

'No.'

'But I can see it.'

'See what?'

'Your you-know-what.'

'Uglebug.'

'Fine,' I said. 'Just help me find Mum. She's not in the garden.'

'Bedroom?' Derek gripped the side of the box, so it curved beneath his fingers, and lifted a leg over the edge. It came down with a stamp.

'Why'd she be in bed?'

'She's always in bed.'

'Only when she's ill.'

'She's always ill.'

'Fine.' I pulled up the corner of the carpet with my heel. Underneath was a decapitated Lego man. 'Let's check upstairs.'

'Why?'

'You said she was upstairs.'

Derek wandered towards the couch, chewing his little finger. 'Who?'

'Mummy. Need to ask her something.'

'Oh.' Derek threw a cushion behind him as he searched for Blankey. The remote followed. 'Why do I have to come?'

The blanket was draped over the fruit bowl on the table. I picked it up and

---

5   Every few months or so, the lock on the cage would snap and I'd be woken by the screams of the chickens.

6   Not that my mother didn't try to throw a party. She even joined an ex-pat Bible Club. Her role was to sit in the corner and nod into her tea as people talked around her.

squeezed it into a ball behind my back. 'Because.'

He turned in a semi-circle, looking from the couch to the remote to the couch. 'Because?'

'Uglebug,' I said.

He shrugged and tugged his cock.

Two weeks later, I told everyone at school that our stairs were haunted. I'd seen a screaming woman and George Wickham from 'Pride and Prejudice.' Daisy Skinner didn't believe me and spent the night on my bedroom floor to prove it. I lay next to her on my parents' blow up bed. I'd wanted to make a pillow wall between us so that she wouldn't curl into my side again. Instead, I balanced myself on the edge and tucked the duvet under me. She was in the middle of the bed when she screamed.

She'd tugged the duvet over our heads and writhed and whimpered till she found me. Her knee hit mine and fingers grabbed at my elbows.

'He's here. They're all here,' she said.

'Who?' I could feel her breath against my shoulder blades.

'Them. Them. We're gonna die.' She coughed into my ear and then went still.

The house was ten years old and built on Henri's first chicken pen. As I tried to shove her corpse off me, I wondered what we'd done to upset them. I'd quit eating meat after Bambi.[7]

After ten minutes, Daisy gave up and wriggled to the cold side of the bed, where she stayed for most of the night, moving only to kick me in the thigh.[8]

Daisy couldn't piss alone. Whenever she needed to go, Maiyu or I would have to follow. She'd shake her knickers down and I would stand facing the corner while she called me a pussy. I stopped going to the toilet at school. I'd stand up and several other girls would follow me. They'd stand at the mirror, brushing their hair and adjusting their earrings, asking me questions about which boy was the cutest and who I'd take to the disco. I'd pull my trousers down and spend a minute staring at my trainers before flushing the empty toilet and answering their question. 'They're just boys.'

'They're not just boys,' Maiyu said. 'They're super-hot, attractive boys.'

'You do like boys, don't you?' Daisy wound her hair around her hand and squeezed it into a curl.[9]

'Some of them. Just not our lot.' I could have listed most of my crushes off for them – James from Team Rocket, Tony Blair, Katherine Howard, Stephen Fry,

---

7   The next morning, I found out that 'them' referred to Henry VIII and his seven wives.

8   That year I saw a ghost for every time Daisy lied.

9   Daisy had three admirers. A boy in Spain, a kid in year three and Joe the football captain. Joe left candy and teddies on her desk and slid love letters into her coat pocket. Daisy had laid them all on her bedroom floor for me. I said I could never imagine a guy doing the same for me. She agreed and told me to keep a teddy.

Mr Peters the Maths teacher, but I'd have stopped before I reached Dami.

Dami was a year younger than me and a foot taller. He was a Nigerian and his Show and Tell object was always a shirtless photo of himself on a beach. It was taken before his operation so you could still see his umbilical hernia poking out of his abdomen. I saw his new navel when he played the lead in the school play. It was a slit.

He'd worn the typical Tarzan outfit. Leopard prints, a skirt and a diagonal strap across the shoulder. One of the Mums had made it.[10] Dami was one of those kids that always got a leading role; the year before he'd been the Rat King in *The Pied Piper* and at Christmas he'd been Joseph. When I crushed on him, he was Mowgli out of *The Jungle Book*. I was the robber who beat his parents to death.[11]

The curtains would open. Jade and Hamish, cradling their newborn blanket, would walk across the stage. When they reached the spotlight, five of us would run down the aisles and hit the air above them with imaginary sticks until the actors remembered to collapse. We'd then hide in the Chorus for the rest of the play.[12] We were never arrested. Instead, I got to sit and watch Dami for two hours a night. I noticed how he stood facing the audience – legs apart, hands on hips. He had the body language thing all worked out.

On our end of year science test he wrote that rice was a liquid and that mammals had cold blood. He couldn't draw a cat and thought 'verb' was French for green, but he could tell you all about method acting.

'It's, like, remembering what it felt like. Remembering what you did,' he said as we ate our packed lunches on the climbing frame steps. 'So, like, crying, yeah. When I cry my face all screws up.'

'Like this?'

'Like that. So, like, when Mowgli's crying over Baloo, I'm thinking. I'm going "hmm, what happened when my hamster died?" Oh *yeah*. My face screwed up. See. Everyone thinks I'm crying.'

'You're really great.' I swallowed my crusts and wiped my fingers on my coat pocket. 'At acting.'

---

10   The same five participated in every event the school held. From concerts to bake sales to World Book Day. They'd come in for every play. They'd make the sets, throw in the plastic props and dress us up in handmade outfits.

11   I'd auditioned for Bagheera. I'd read the book, seen the movie and I'd made a fucking character analysis sheet. He's the serious and responsible opposite to Baloo's carefree, don't-give-a-shit attitude. See, this is when I was serious about being an actor. Did they go for the canonical interpretation of the character? Shit no. He became some Baloo rip-off. He spoke in one-liners and made his entrance moonwalking down the stage.

12   The Chorus sat on three rows at the back of the stage. Everyone had been banned from going backstage so, whenever a scene finished, the characters would turn around and sit next to the animal most likely to eat them. The head, Raj, claimed this was because he wanted the jungle to look like it was full of animals and sixty chorus members did not make a jungle. He had no problem with five robbers and two murder victims sitting and singing with the giraffes and the alligators.

He shrugged and emptied his lunchbox in the bin. 'Gonna play footie today?'

'Yeah.'

'Good one, mate. Be right back.' He nodded goodbye and ran into the crowds of children, dodging the British Bulldog players and scooting around the kids trading cards.

'You like him then.' Daisy had thumped down beside me.

'He can act.'

She'd twisted to face me, slamming her hand against the step next to my head. 'You said you didn't like boys.'

'No I didn't.'

'You meant it.'

'What?'

'You can't take him to the disco.'

'He's going?'

'You said you'd go with me. And Maiyu.'

'I am.'

'Good. Girls stick together. Boys are dumb.' She wrapped her fingers around my hand. 'They can't be friends with girls.'

Before I turned the corner that led to my parents' room, I tried to rehearse the question but found that I didn't have one. I knew there was something but not what that something should be. There were crushes, there was sex, there were discos, and there were boys and friends and girls.[13]

I'd start by saying that Daisy and I had had another fight. She'd ask why and I'd have to tell her about Dami. I'd work backwards until I came to the elephants.

By this time I was in-front of my parents' door. It was shut. Even at night it was never shut. To shut it was to shut the air out, and, when the air was shut out, the mould would grow, and the windowsill would rot.

I held the door handle for five minutes, not twisting it or pulling it. This would be the moment in one of Dad's novels when the story would get going. Poirot would come round and tut as we hid evidence and contradicted ourselves. There were questions that needed to be asked.

I should have asked questions when Marguerite, our landlord's wife, discovered Easter the rabbit dead. We'd been on holiday to a caravan park in Pembrokeshire, and when we came back I was missing a rabbit. She'd been buried in the garden. Marguerite couldn't remember where.

Patch died nearly a year later. I'd come back from school and found her lying in her hutch. I'd reached out to stroke her but she didn't run away or bite, just

---

13   I already knew about kissing. When I was seven, I kissed Aaron Watts on the mouth after he asked me to be his girlfriend. He said we should stick to kissing cheeks and never spoke to me again.

let me run my fingers through her fur. Under it her stomach was tight, drawn close to the bone. The food bowl was full. It'd been full that morning too. I'd refilled it and peeled the straw off the floor of the hutch. The new straw was now matted with balls of shit. Yellowy-white lumps wriggled amongst it. I lifted up Patch's tail. Above her arse was a damp, pink hole.

The vet didn't speak English and my Mum knew little Dutch, so they compromised and spoke French. I sat at the back of the room and repeated all the French phrases I knew.

'Je mal à la tête. La petite grenouille est verte. La gomme s'il vous plaît. Derrière. Merde. Baise-moi.'

My Mum sat next to me. 'She's in a lot of pain.'

'He's going to murder her, isn't he?'

'He's going to put her down.'

'I don't want him to.'

'If he doesn't she'll die at home.' She rested her hand on my knee. 'It'd be very long and painful for her.'

'No.'

'All he's going to do is give her a little injection.'

'There's no such thing.'

'She'll fall asleep. It's a lovely way to go. The best way to go.'

'No. No.'

I didn't watch her die. I sat in the waiting room and cried. I attracted a small circle of Dutch people. They patted my arms and knees and chattered away and tried to introduce me to their pets. I rested my face on Patch and Easter's travel cage and told them that 'I don't speak Dutch, I don't speak Dutch. I hate cats and I don't speak Dutch. Je suis Anglais.'

My mum brought Patch out in a shoebox. We carried her to where Derek and Dad sat eating burgers in the car and drove her home.

'We shouldn't have taken them out to Belgium,' Mum said when we buried Patch. 'It just makes them ill. It's the climate.'

'I want a drink.' Derek rattled the stairway gate. 'I'm thirsty.'

Still holding the handle to my parents' door, I peeked through the keyhole. The curtains were open and lipsticks lay collapsed on the dressing table. 'Mummy, Derek's thirsty.'

Outside, the chickens squawked and ran, their wings beating against their bodies.

Mum didn't answer.

She could be wrapping Derek's birthday presents. If I was to open the door now, I'd see her grappling with the sticky-tape. In fifty-nine minutes she'd be thinking about cooking dinner. I'd come back then and knock and, if that didn't get a reply, I'd call out. But I couldn't do it now. I didn't open the door.

White Dust / *Timothy Williams*

No nigger was treated bad for no reason. They just acted up a lot more, cause they were different to how they are now. Not all were clean and smart and fair like them you see on the videos. I didn't know one like that mulatto running round saying he should be president, but I heard about them ones though: political pretensions. Snakes in the grass. Hell, I remember a real dirty nigger went for me and my friends once. Savage kid, and crazy too. Damn near killed a few of us, and got hanged for it as I remember.

Me and the gang were taking a break on the drive back from Crossett market – Stan had his pa's car again. Me and two boys, David and Skinny Henry, were crammed in the back with only Georg and Stan up front. Stan, the driver, was older'n us, so just old enough to be trusted with the car, but slow-minded and heavy-moving, so he was little use to his pa in the store. We were big for those times, all somehow spared too much of a young working life, even through the depression and the black blizzards.

Whether it was cause of the heat, or cause of a long drive stuffed up next to Skinny Henry, we stopped by a farm and out came this nigger yelling at us. 'You pigs,' 'you dogs,' 'you idiot sons of monkeys and whores,' 'you fuckin bay'stards, I have kids....'

He spat at Georg, and then I reckon Georg pushed him away, told him to leave, but the nigger hit him. I swore I was so surprised. No nigger should ever try stuff on Georg. Hell, I'm not sure anyone should of tried to hit Georg back then, coloured or not. Everyone knew his pa was part of the Mississippi plan, knew he drove the whole family a bit crazy before he died and they headed west.

So the nigger got beat back and told to respect us that run things, but instead of seeing what he'd done wrong, and running or crying, the nigger started beating Georg harder. I mean, imagine, with us four others there and everything and this nigger thought he'd start a fight? He was a fiery nigger, sure, and landed a few sore hits on me, but no nigger's good enough for the five of us. We were doing good, getting him back, even knocked him to the floor, but I think he found some branch and beat us all down low before running off. Something like that anyway. I thought he was leaving so I let him be and turned to see if Stan, who took the worst, was alright down on the floor, but he was just dusty, sweating and laughing, white patches of dust blotching his smiling face, too dumb to feel the pain yet.

It must have been then the sneaky nigger hit me from behind, hard, over the forehead with some tire iron that he must of found. I went out real brief and all I could do when I came back was listen and watch what little I could. One figure beating the others with first the iron and then some metal chain.

Eventually us five... I think we got him pinned – each taking a limb while Georg fetched a sheriff or some lawman who took away the nigger.... In the end I heard some judge ruled that he should be strung up from a tree by the entrance to his farm.

I know it sounds bad now but to crazy niggers like that it was the only way to tell them what way to act was right and what way was wrong. You just don't know how the world was back then.

Thing is I remember something more now. It started as just one little moment. There was loads of us all sort of lined up, drinking water and yelling to each other. Then through the middle, as if we'd formed up with a gap for them to go by, came men in all white. They shone, you know? They held a fancy cross with battery-powered lights running up and across it and everyone else was just a shadow of a face or a gut or a boot but they were clear and white and so *clean*.

Now I remember, they talked. And they were right. They were so obviously *right*. And I weren't expecting that. I was there for some friend. Reckon it was Georg. Might a been Stan. But these men in white were holding that cross or holding the good book and talking to us like a friend with a message of *truth* and they was *shining*. My thighs were damn near soaked and I reckon muddy but they was *still* shining white and fine up on a low stage, only a head above us all now we'd moved to be shoulder on shoulder facing them, them just white triangle heads speaking. And we *knew* they was right. We knew what they was saying before they said it cause it was in our hearts. Damn, they should've been preachers.

That ain't all either. These guys were a part of everything. They did meetings at farms all over the place and if the season was bad, or if they felt like it, in churches or houses too. They *understood* people. They helped us to understand *why* we were so mad – what we were mad *at*.

They'd say, 'Them niggers are uncivilised. It ain't their fault, but it's true. That's a fact. It's *biology*. Now, knowing that, we must protect ourselves from barbaric idiots gaining power over us, cause they ain't nothing but beasts, they ain't nothing *like* people. We must stop them from pushing their uncivilised ways onto us. We *must* keep them from themselves, keep them from holding the ways of beasts over us.'

'Them up north – you know the type, them in law, them in suits and in cities, them in papers saying big words for all America – they think they right but they don't know the south. They don't know what it's like to break sweat before early morning is done, or how beasts are beasts and people are people. They ain't seen how these animals just prove themselves to be animals over and over. They think just cause they can talk some words, cause they shaped like people, that they are people. They say that black is people too. Now, you know what I say? I say I once had a parrot that can talk better than any nigger I met but a bird ain't no man, and I got a cow that's as black as them niggers but that cow's a cow no matter how you dress it.'

See, they knew how to word stuff without it losing sense. They said that we should rule ourselves, that we was smart enough to run our farms and towns with no help from power grabbers up north, and it was true; city brains ain't hard enough for understanding life out there then. They say too how life was worth more way back before they gave our property, our beasts, the same rights as us, how niggers ain't built smart enough to run anything, how the rules the north pushes on us just makes us littler each day. Pretty soon I was headed over to Crossett with Georg and Stan to get ourselves some capped suits of white.

I remember I was riding up front for a change, with Georg stretched out back wanting to lie down, seeing as Skinny Henry was sick and David didn't want a suit of white yet. We went to a local lady's, Mrs Ingram, just down the road from the centre of Crossett, who we was told would take our sizes and then our money. I bet Stan and Georg had rights to money enough for it but I'd had to save and then beg it from my folks. And even then I had to slip a bit extra out the stash when I was alone.

'Did you boys go to the bank to get this money today?' Mrs Ingram was the strong, ugly type. She must of been used to difficult men having raised her four boys, all known from one meet or the other, all strong but skinny — sinewy like old trap horses. She never looked away from her sizing, all the while working at calming our nerves that come from making a big purchase.

'No maam, I guess we all just had it to hand.' Georg leaned at the door lookin in on her measuring Stan.

One way or the other, I said from my seat by the window.

'Well, at least y'all ain't the thieving kind.' My buttocks pinched the wooden chair, my eyes now interested in everything but her. 'Unlike that nigger, robbing ten silver dollars from the bank and only getting tossed in jail for it.'

That was just the sort of conversations we had at meets, setting us more at ease, relaxing my pinch on the chair. She talked to us about the local girls knowing we was all single while measuring Georg and eventually moving onto me, measuring idly the length of arm and breadth of chest as a murmur rose from behind the tree line.

After the sizing we wandered into town, leaving the car with Mrs Ingram, and we found this crowd yammering down near the County Jail Yard. Georg grabbed a shoulder, asked what happened.

'Some jailed negro slashed the marshal, escaped and been caught.'

Stan elbowed through some of the crowd, hands the size of plates reaching back and dragging us up to him, getting us near enough to the centre to see between heads and over shoulders to where a nigger stood in among the mass with a noose round his neck, white dust making him plainer, making wet cuts easier to see. We waited, hearing bigger and bigger tales of what he'd done.

'FRANK TURNER.' One call from a man near the nigger killed all speculating. 'You have been jailed for stealing silver from the bank and have now slashed the man in charge of enforcing your punishment for that aforementioned.' I recognised the voice from the meets. 'Seeing as you injured the law, it now falls on us to punish you.'

'Hang him,' some cried.

'He's a murderer.'

'Slash him first,' I yelled.

People up front had started pushing again, jabbing the nigger with fingers, spitting on him. He was pushed down to his knees. The man with the big voice yanked him back up and hauled him over to the wall, then handed the rope of the noose to another man. More people spat, shouted, slapped and hit the nigger. He cried out through it all, nothing but garbage, words lost to sobs that proved his guilt. The rope was slung over a pipe and he was pulled from the ground. Someone cheered as he stopped twitching.

You see these guys didn't just talk, they acted too. They had fingers in big politics as well as local lives. We heard stories of righteous, local, active justice in other states from the papers. It didn't matter that the marshal wasn't dead – that nigger had proved himself bad.

Soon enough our whites were ready and we took our places in the big outdoors events. We took to our parts and moved always a little too slow or late, then a little too fast or early, and slowly saw the cross aflame until it wasn't nothing but ash and stump.

After that it wasn't just them talking at us. We all talked for hours in all the groups that came. All of us suddenly friends now knowing we were all mad in the same way, that somehow we all the same and different from those out there. I discovered that being called Ben is a good thing. That it makes me a natural member because of some sort of thing in Hollywood with D. W. Griffith back just afore I was born. I discovered that everyone knew I'd fall in love with a girl called 'Elsie,' but that no-one knew where I'd find her. I should say now that I didn't know about Hollywood's first great film back then. I ain't even sure I'd seen one movie, but I knew they existed. Back then everyone seemed to have seen 'A Birth of a Nation' but me. I never really remembered who I talked to or what the others were doing, I just kept talking until I'd run out of things to say, then I'd move on to another group. Turns out while I wandered about, Georg got busy getting a little popular and was even, eventually, taken to assist in talking to ignorant men, as we once were.

We went to everything the first few months, cramming into Stan's car for anywhere too far to walk to, staying out late, never working the next day. David took a habit of vanishing after we got our capped suits of white and after the second or third week of us going he stopped turning up to everything we did, even when he says 'yer, sure, I'll be there.'

Skinny Henry tried the hardest; he used to get us all to go over to David's pa's place to try and get him to come out. Every time we went for him he just acted odd about us turning up on his pa's land, his pa standing behind him, arms crossed and never moving, his ma and two young sisters poking their heads round the doorframe to steal glances of us, bug-eyed but cautious. What scared them? I ain't sure even now that I know. We knew they were Jews, but they were farmers like us, struggling like us. They were just another family. Not them money-taking Jew immigrants we heard about, but, you know, with them hiding from us like that I started to wonder whether there was more to it...

After that Skinny Henry started to actually get skinny. Lost more weight in three months than most men own. My folks said his family farm was having a tough year, that ours could be better if I put more time in, and soon enough Skinny Henry stopped having the time to do much else but work. The failing land ate him up as far as we knew.

Eventually the war swallowed Stan whole but spit me back out into an America where my folks owned nothing and lived off charity. I had to find work elsewhere to live by.

That mark on my forehead from where that nigger hit me with the tire iron – it ain't what I thought it was like. I found it just now, smoother than I remember it being last I found it, but I can still tell it was sharp like from a corner, not flat like from a shaft. Like I got caught by the iron coming down from above and in front of me, but the nigger got me from behind with the flat part. I know that. I can see it.

I was just thinking today about how those suits of white seem nowadays, and I remembered something new. Way back, when Stan's Pa made a good run of sales from some throw-away tyres, selling them on to some out of town garage, Stan found himself with some money for helping out. Thing is a man like Stan didn't know what to do with it and was too dumb to see the point in stashing it. The day before a meet in a Johnson's field, a couple miles out of town, just too long to make walking worth goin, he says to Georg and me to meet him on the road in front of Georg's if we want a lift. So we're standing there, looking southwest toward an orange sun, knowing he'd come round the corner from that way. Both of us too hot to be in our suits of white yet, so just holding them balled up under an arm, not caring if people know we're part of it now.

A white cloud of dust started kicking up behind the rise where the road came from and soon enough the rattling car wheeled round the corner. But something just didn't look right and both Georg and me stood silent, staring at it, trying to figure out what we was seeing. It looked like Stan driving with a dust cover still over it, but the cover had holes that seemed to sort of fit the windows. As it bounced closer I saw his left arm out the window, holding the cover down to the bonnet, stopping it riding up over the windscreen, and then there it all was, stopping in front of us. He got out, chest held big and proud, and he walked round the car fixing the sheet so that all the holes fitted right over all the windows again. He'd gone and spent his money on a full suit of white for the car. A bad suit of white too. It was already torn and stained near the wheels, one side seemed longer than the other, the cap of the suit – God alone knew what he thought would fill it – hung back all limp like a tail, and a big red cross on each side made it look like one of them ambulances.

'Well, ain't we gonna be loved tonight?' Stan said, leaning on the bonnet, all smile and no shame.

I swear that's the hardest I laughed that year. Georg eventually convinced him not to use it ever again, and so on the way to the meet we detoured to some local nigger farm and hung it over the tree by the entrance to their land.

Shit. I remember who he was and all – that nigger that attacked us when we were younger. Gus. Just some nigger that took over his daddy's farm and took a hand to running a store instead of farming for us to sell. Was taking all the black business from Stan's pa's store in town. Was doing too good off it and word had him buying a motor car. Too fuckin big for his boots. Man, we hated him. No wonder I didn't care he hanged.

I can see him busy with fixing a wire fence for hens and us five going down from the road into his farm to see him. Must of wanted to talk to him bout something.

No.

I can see now Georg spitting in Gus's face. Gus pushing Georg and telling us to leave, not spitting back at Georg. I can see Georg hitting him, white dust rising as all six of us move.

I can see David and Skinny Henry holding him up by the arms. I can see me punching him held there and the flecks of spittle flying as he cried out at us. I can hear Stan telling him what he was doing to white men and his pa's store. Georg telling him that makes him a pig, a monkey becoming a pig, a monkey becoming a dog that needs to be kicked. It was then that Gus spat in Georg's face. I can see Georg walking off a sec and coming back with a branch, hitting his gut.

'You fuckin bay'stards, I's got kids.'

I can see Georg kick him where it'd hurt and telling Stan to get ready to punch the nigger down to where he deserves then telling the other two to let him go. I can see Stan swinging and missing the falling nigger's face – the nigger crumpling still from Georg's last kick – and Stan stumbling side-on then falling, and rolling, and ending up lying on his back, facing the sky, that white dust visible all over him, sweating and laughing. I can hear the nigger's cries blending with our laughs.

I can see Georg back with a tire iron and a chain, lording out law-like phrases bout theft and assault. I can see black flesh turning dark red from the hits. I can see bleeding black feet and calves. I can see the chain swinging from my arm into his chest. I can see Georg beside me striking side-on into calve and catching my forehead swinging back up. I remember my head ringing as I tried to laugh it off and stay holding down the nigger.

I can see my hands round the nigger's arm while blinking away blood, doing what Georg said, not backing down, being a man. Standing with Stan and the other two in a square around the weak nigger, us all taking a limb while Georg put a rope over the nigger's head and looked up at a tree.

I can't see us hanging him. We was just young. I can remember the look David and Skinny Henry each gave Georg when he looked up at the tree, their thoughts and strengths fading. I can hear Georg's voice saying 'Learn from this you dumb, shit-coloured dog. We have to come here again, I might decide to test how strong this rope is.'

But that doesn't explain seeing a rope loop over a beam, seeing black ankles with red, brown and grey soles being lifted, shaking, from the ground. Nor why my throat wants to cheer at that memory.

Absolute / *Genevieve Allen*

22nd August

She bought new shoes today. She didn't intend to, they just caught her eye as she walked past the window. Ten minutes later I watched her smile as she stood in front of the shop mirror, testing how they felt, getting used to the height of the heel, the pressure on the ball of her foot, how tight she needed the straps. Dark plum suede, half-inch wedge at the front, three-and-a-half-inch heel, thin strap with a buckle around each of her ankles – outlandish, for her.

25th August

Absorbed in her novel, she lifted a finger to nibble her nail. I've started to do it too. The more I see her do it, the more I seem to copy. She'd painted her nails a bright apple green that looked like it belonged on a kitchen wall. But the varnish was imperfect, chipped by her teeth and dissolved by dishwater.

    I shifted on the park bench. It was a fairly new one; the slats still smooth, not splintered and creaking like most of the others. It was as yet undecorated with scratches of postcodes and phone numbers and marker pen declarations of eternal love. I felt her shift too, crossing her legs tighter and rolling her shoulders. Her elbow clicked. She started to twitch her leg – that thing people do that they forget other people can feel, where they jog their leg against the floor. I smiled. She didn't notice. That was something I liked about her: how unobservant she was while reading.

29th August

Today, we returned to the gallery. My favourite thing about our gallery visits are the shoes she wears: always heels, still sensible. That's her. Today it's the brown leather pair, tan really, with laces, decorative holes punched along the edges and a two-inch heel. Sometimes she wears the suede olive green court shoes with the two-and-a-half inch heel. They make a better noise. The clack of her sensible heels is our relationship. Clack *click* clack *click*. A metronome. My guide. The rhythm she sets for me, a constant ticking, keeps me in time, helps me find the way.

    The gallery is the best place to listen to her heels; old buildings have marvellous acoustics. The floors are tiled, a chill off-white that looks both dirty and clean. And on them, my beauty's feet sing. I can close my eyes and know exactly where she is in the room. She wanders through white pillars, cherubs carved in corners, all smiles, swirls, and clouds – ticks on a Georgian architect's check list. The ceilings are high above her head. The rooms are all long, stretched and rectangular – they make her look insignificantly small – and the doors, marked by pillars and architraves, remind me of the entrances to temples.

    She stops at one of her favourite paintings. I know it's one of her favourites because she always smiles at it. A tiny smile she forgets to hide for a few seconds. It makes little lines around her lips. The painting's of a girl; she is delicate and wispy like she's made of tissue paper. She's clutching a King ChArlès spaniel in her spindly hands. The dog is looking at us, out of the frame, an expression of distaste and inevitability on its squashed-up face, as if it's about to roll its eyes.

We walk into the next room. *Click* clack *click*. She sits on the bench in the middle. She always sits by this painting the longest. She doesn't want to get in the other visitors' way. It's a Stubbs painting – *Horse Attacked By Lion*. She likes Stubbs. Every time we go to a gallery she'll try to buy a Stubbs postcard from the gift shop. I don't like it much, but I'd never tell her that. I like the eyes he paints though. They stand out. They pop white-yellow and stare around.

18th September

I bought flowers for her birthday. Orange and white lilies. They clash with her hair, but they remind me of her. I left the card blank.

19th September

**ABSOLUT
RASPBERRI**
Feel the rich and intense
burst of flavours blended with
vodka distilled from grain grown
in the rich fields of southern Sweden.
The distilling and flavouring of vodka
is an age-old Swedish tradition
dating back more than 400 years.
Vodka has been sold under the name
Absolut since 1879.

12th October

We sat in the park again today. The air was dry and heavy, full of late pollen and the smell of dead leaves. Around us, children laughed and blew dandelion clocks in each other's faces. We didn't talk. I just watched her read, listening as her finger ran the grainy length of the pager edge, flipping it to read on. The words can make her smile or frown if they want to. Sometimes they make her cry. Could I make her smile? Could I make her cry?

15th October

Infusion
Eau de Toilette

This exotic floral
eau de toilette
envelops you in
sheer freesia,
seduces you with
gardenia and
intrigues you with
mysterious orchid,
leaving you a heart
of rich amber and
vanilla. Infusion is
your gateway to
the Orient.
AVOID CONTACT
WITH THE EYES.
STORE IN A COOL
DARK PLACE.

18th October

Epic and poetic, this Wonder Tale is classic
Kneehigh stuff. Charting a life from child to adult.
You can expect instinctive storytelling and a heady
mix of live blues music and devilish humour.
The Wild Bride is a grown-up, spring bud, dustball
of a romance for adults and brave children alike.
www.kneehigh.co.uk

27th October

We went to the theatre today. I like our theatre trips almost as much as our gallery
trips; they're very atmospheric. The lighting isn't much to my liking – I can't see her
well. I like to think I can sense her – a sigh, a stirring in her seat – but certainly I can
smell hairspray and Chanel. And I can hear her. In the vast space around us, I can hear
sweet wrappers and shoes – the scuffling and scraping of students in for the matinee
performance – but I only listen to her. She sits still, looking at the curtained stage,
rolling a throat sweet around with her tongue. I was with her when she bought them

earlier. I imagine they make her breath taste of cherries and menthol.

The curtain rises and a bluesy, drawling melody makes me think of dust and empty spaces. Teachers shush their students, and, as the actors begin, the last mobiles beep farewell.

The play is wild, elemental, full of warnings and hard-earned happily-ever-afters. A folk tale. The heroine's father has accidentally sold her to the devil, but he can't take her yet. All through her life he's waiting for her to slip up. She walks in the wilderness, the Devil lurking at every crossroads, under every stone and up every tree. At every turn you fear he'll get her for good. But she eludes him, and stays safe with her prince and her happy ending.

She claps, I clap, we clap, and I wonder why every person in the audience looks so happy the devil lost.

5th November

Remember, remember.

We watched the fireworks together this evening, bumped and nudged by anonymous scarf-wrapped spectators. Around a large bonfire, children clutched sparklers in gloved fingers, as if each holding a small fairy. Their breaths plumed and dissipated in air thick with wood smoke and the smell of caramelising sugar. I watched as the sparks in the sky lit her face green, pink and gold.

6th November

We had to go to the supermarket today. She needed more bread: golden seed loaf 500g. I walked behind her, watching the basket swing on her arm, looking up when she stopped to inspect a label or weigh an item in her palm. Her hair still smelt like wood smoke and gunpowder from last night. She had just rounded the corner of the dairy aisle to move into bread, when she shouted 'eggs,' turned sharply, and walked back the way she had come.

She walked into me.

Her eyes – bronze eyeshadow, green irises – flicked up to my face, and she apologised with a small smile.

She smiled at me.

Smiled. At me.

She's never smiled at me before. I've seen her smile. And laugh, and frown, and cry, and roll her eyes every time her friend Lydia is late when they meet for coffee. But she's never smiled *at me* before.

For once, I didn't count the items she put through the checkout, calculate how much she had spent, or note how many bags she'd used. I'm sorry I didn't now. I feel restless, as if I've left something half finished. Maybe I should go over and see her… but what if she doesn't want to see me?

10th November

Carte Noire is enjoyed in France for its unique aroma and flavour.

The sensual pleasure of pure
Arabica coffee captured
in the intense aroma of
Carte Noire has been preserved
in this deeply aromatic Décaféiné
blend. Rich and velvety in body,
Carte Noire will seduce *your* body.

Kraft Foods UK

11th November

We stood together in as near to silence as a large group of people can get – a sneeze or cough, a sniff as an older lady tried to check her tears, a rustle of poppies, the stamping wellies of a child too young to understand. But then my girl raised her hand to scratch the back of her neck, just on her hairline, and I caught the scent of the perfume she wears in winter; it is fruity and spicy, like Christmas cake.

The silence almost over, I felt the crowd starting to bubble, getting ready to speak again. Then I was nervous. Would she turn and see me? Look straight at me? Straight through me? I couldn't decide which would be worse. I want her to see me, I want her to know that I'm here for her and her only, but I'm not yet ready for her to know how much she means to me.

21st November

We stood by the sea for hours, as the wind grew stronger, seeking to tear buttons from their holes. She likes to do this sometimes, when she doesn't know what else to do. She likes to sit, or stand, by the sea, and just look at it. Tide in, tide out, waves break, roll back out, rip tide, current, blue-grey-green. I imagine she thinks it gives her some sort of clarity, detachment, perspective.

Half a mile inland, the village glowed as evening seeped around us. She rubbed her hands up and down her arms, to bring warmth or comfort or both. Her boots had grey, flat soles and their insides were lined with thinning fake fur. I couldn't smell her perfume – the wind was stealing the scent.

Surely, I thought, the time is right *now*? But there's so much I... So many things could go wrong. But since that day in the supermarket, when she showed me her smile – *me* – I'd had doubts about my waiting. Patience is important, I thought, but some things can't wait for forever. So I walked towards her, towards the sea. What if she knows? I thought. What if she knows before I even say anything? I couldn't feel my hands.

I stopped.

I was standing beside her.

After a moment, she turned towards me, and for a second we stood face to face in the evening dark. I inhaled to speak as the wind fought to stop me.

'Hello.'

She looked surprised: her eyes widened, and then a small frown settled on her forehead.

Yes, I thought, this is it. She knows. She *has* to know.

Every inch, every pore, every cell of my body was pulsing, waiting for that look of recognition, waiting for that look of reciprocation.

'Hi,' she said.

Then she turned.

She walked back up the beach, stumbling slightly on the wet shingle. Far away, a ship's horn sounded, and seagulls squawked in white circles. For the first time in months, I didn't follow her.

She doesn't know me.

December 9th

It hasn't snowed yet this year, but everyone smells of de-icer. Everything is red, or gold, and covered in glitter. I saw her today, in the shoe shop at the back of the shopping centre. I stopped to watch her at the till, smiling and chatting to the shop assistant, clutching a smooth shoebox in her arms. For a moment, I thought I could smell her perfume, and imagined the shoes she would have inside that box, and the sound they would make as she ascended the shopping centre stairs.

But I walked on, back straight and hands in pockets, and all around me, in the shop windows, on shining decorations and behind my closed eyelids, there glowed a thousand reflections of my own smile.

Rubik's Cube / *Jessica Lawrence*

Fifty-four squares of colour jumbled up. I can turn the rows for hours and still not make the faces match. Three whites are lined up. I turn them to meet two white faces but in the process I split the greens. When *you* work the cube, I feel strangely emasculated. 'Right across, left inverted, down, right,' you mutter, your fingers obeying. I feel some trait of masculinity should equip me to do this sort of thing, but I can't. I just twist the rows and columns haphazardly. I turn the pieces and hope I make the right move.

Four blues share the same face. Blue is the seaside on October 11th. The sea was cold and the wind powerful but you and I still rolled up our trousers and raced to the water. I ran faster but let you win. You always liked to win against me, a trait I enjoyed except when you lost. A red square sits solitary on the left but I turn the whole cube until it's out of sight. Red is your temper. Red is an argument that blossoms from nowhere. To me, a lie is telling a deliberate untruth with the intent to deceive someone. For you, just the omission of a detail is a lie. Saying 'I'm fine' when I'm not is a lie to you. Have you counted how many times we've argued over that?

Start with green, you always told me. Make that face 'match and work from there. Green is Coleway Park. It was summer and the sun was just about bearable with the breeze. We stood beneath a willow tree, the light falling on us in intermittent rays as the wind pushed through the limp branches. Your tears stained my T-shirt and you spoke only five words that day. 'Sandy's dead,' were the first two, said as I met you at the entrance. I never cared a great deal for your dog. She yapped too much in that annoying manner of Yorkshire terriers and she growled whenever I was near. You found it funny; I found it irritating. Still, I would have kissed Sandy from nose to tail to be able to go back and hear you say those final three words again. 'I love you.'

I try incredibly hard to follow your advice but the Coleway Park squares won't meet. Every time I see this cube on my table I strive to make the nine greens share one face. You think I don't put in the effort; I see it in your expression each time you spot the unfinished cube on my coffee table. I once read about the mating ritual of a particular bird species (I forget which one): in this species, the female will only mate with a male who has perfectly memorised her unique song. When you see my unfinished cube, you press your lips together and arch your right brow, as though you sense my failure at some evolutionary level. Who would have thought that one look could embody so much?

I ignore green and play around with yellow instead. Yellow is July 3rd. I was in town for no real purpose other than to enjoy the sunshine. A stall caught my attention, laden with puzzles and gadgets. I studied the items for a while before the vendor held something out to me: a cube with six coloured faces. As he explained the complex ways of the cube I saw that someone else was listening in. The way the sun touched the yellow tulip in your hair... I hadn't noticed I was staring until you removed your sunglasses and I found your eyes on mine.

'I'll take one of those cubes,' you said, 'but only if this gentleman does, too.'

'How can I refuse now?' I replied, wishing I had something wittier to say. You seemed satisfied, nonetheless. We each paid the vendor but you took my cube from him before I could, handing me your own.

'Shuffle it for me?' you asked, already taking it upon yourself to scramble mine. I separated the colours of your cube, twisting and turning the same amount of times you twisted and turned mine. I stopped when you did and we exchanged; the toy looked more intimidating in its scrambled form that it had before.

'Thanks.'

'Tell you what,' you said, producing a small white card from the pocket of your shorts, 'call me when you complete it.'

That was two years ago. Still the cube remains incomplete. I twist the left row upwards. Two whites and our first date. You agreed to meet me even though I hadn't fulfilled your task. I still remember that speech you gave me when I baulked at your plans for our evening, but the title of the rom-com you insisted on is forgotten.

'No one loves like the characters in films anymore. No one is as romantic and impulsive as they are. I mean leaving flowers on the doorstep with no card so she guesses who they're from but doesn't know for sure, that's what half the romance is: uncertainty. Does he like me? Did he mean to brush my hand as we walked to the restaurant? When was the last time you saw a guy chase a girl through the airport to declare his love? That doesn't happen anymore. It's sad. Those corny lines at the end where they finally realise that what kept them apart at first is so trivial compared to their love. Sure we might cringe at how clichéd it is but what girl can honestly say she doesn't want a guy like George Bailey who will lasso the moon for her?'

After that, I was nervous for the whole date. Should I buy you flowers? Should I take your hand? Did you want me to rustle up a corny phrase for when I walked you home? You got me thinking about every move, every word, every action and wondering how you were interpreting it all.

I turn the top row to the right and reveal an orange between two blues. Remember my birthday when you baked a cupcake for each year of my life and drizzled them with orange icing? We ate so much that day I thought I'd never stand up again.

Right across, left inverted, down, right. That lone red square is on top again. I twist it back and two more take its place.

Red is the last two months. I know what words you want to hear, the same three that you spoke at Coleway Park. It's not that I don't want to say them; it's that I want to say more than they can manage.

'If ever our fate rested on you giving a speech we'd all be doomed,' you'd say. We would laugh but it was true. The words for how I care have yet to find a voice but they're in my heart. It isn't indifference, you see; take my word for that.

Right, left, up inverted, left. Hopeless. This cube will never be completed. I set it down on my coffee table at the sound of the front door opening. Only you have a key. It's been a week since I saw you and I start to smile but your frown stops me. You hold up my key. 'I just came to return this.'

'Right. You can leave it on the table.'

You set it down beside my cube. I watch your fingers linger next to the puzzle before you pick it up and turn it about. Three blues on top and seagulls cry. The next face shows a couple of greens and the smell of blossom on the willow fills the room. Two yellows together, a daffodil drinking in the sunshine. One more turn and the red cube is on top.

Red is love. It's taking the cube and shuffling it before I even have the chance to hold it. It's the way you removed your sunglasses like you were some kind of movie star. The way you pulled the card from your pocket.

As you start to twist the rows of colours into order my thoughts line up coherently. You start on the greens and I start to speak. 'I have a lot that I want to say to you but my thoughts are shuffled and they don't always come out. I wish that I could always say the perfect things or give you an answer that makes you smile.'

You don't look at me but I can tell that you're listening.

'I wish that I could express myself better, but when I try to say something – something important – my thoughts are all jumbled up.' I look at you, not at what your hands are doing. Your face is what brings these words out. 'In all those rom-coms we've watched, the guy tells the girl he loves her in some magical, romantic way.'

You place the cube down on the table and look at me. 'So…?'

My eyes seek the cube beside my keys. Fifty-four squares of colour lined up. 'I'm like a Rubik's cube,' I say, 'and you complete me.'

Polished Oak / *Rebecca Edwards*

'Don't look at the coffin. Don't think about it,' says your mother. 'Just read your speech – it'll be lovely.'

You have never liked the idea of coffins – it doesn't make sense to you, to put a body in a box made of dead tree – and you shift along the pew and rest your cheek on your mother's shoulder. 'I'm scared,' you whisper.

'What of?'

'I don't want to speak anymore.'

'Just ignore the coffin. You'll be fine. Don't think about it.'

You suppose that your mother doesn't look at the coffin because it's how she learnt to deal with her father's death – your grandfather's – when she had to attend his funeral. She, like you, was taken out of school for the day, was woken early and dressed in black mourning clothes, which had been folded neatly at the foot of her bed the night before. Maybe it was easier for her to stare at the back of the pew, to examine dark wood the colour of plain chocolate.

Your foot collides with the back of the bench and makes a loud thud, causing the gentle hum of hushed conversation behind you to pause. You duck your head, feeling heat rise gradually from the base of your neck until it touches your ear lobes. Putting your hand in your pocket and closing your fingers around the piece of paper, you resolve to re-read your scratchy handwriting so you don't get frightened when you have to stand up and speak to the church.

Your fingers quiver as you unfold the paper, which you hold flat in your lap so you don't have to look at the altar. The bumps where you pressed your pen too hard into the paper feel like Braille beneath your fingertips. You pick out words like 'water,' 'paddling pool,' and 'summer' in the loops and lines of dark blue biro, and as you read you remember the smell of grass cuttings and warm water, the smell of your father's skin warmed by the sun as he mowed at the far end of your garden twelve summers ago; he smelled like dried suncream and charcoal and burnt chicken skin. In the corner the barbeque was cooling off and the charcoal was covered in a fine grey dust, and the occasional breeze would sweep a little dust sideways and reveal gaps that glowed bright orange, like flecks of lava. The sun was beginning to fade, streaking the sky pale pink and orange, like the sky in one of your grandmother's water colours.

You were in your tiny paddling pool with your grandma holding your wrists. You must have been three or four, because your sister was still only a baby at the time. You were jumping up and down with the aid of your grandmother; she was lifting you by the wrists and launching you higher into the air with each jump. Droplets of water showered everywhere, as if the paddling pool was a smashed window kicked from below, and your feet slipped and slid on the paddling pool's rubbery floor. Occasionally, your foot caught one of the creases, which formed because your garden was not entirely flat, and looked like little blue worms wriggling underneath the pool.

You were jumping around in circles, spinning through the shadows of a chestnut tree. Its branches were overgrown and covered with brown-green leaves that brushed your shoulders, and the air and water were cool and untouched by the sun. Then you and your grandmother would complete your circle of bounces and be out of the shade of the tree and back in the sun-warmed water, and every time you blinked the sun turned your eyelids translucent, making the vision behind your eyes blood red. The skin on your grandmother's hands felt like an old leather-bound photo album: a safe protective cover for an infinite source of memories.

The organ begins to play, and your mother takes your hand as the people in the church stand up as one, the motion sounding like a deep exhalation. You stare at the wide, black back of the man in front of you, not wanting to look towards the steady shuffle coming from the back of the church.

'Mum?'

'Don't look, Jenny, just don't look.'

Your mother's palm feels hot and slick in your own, so you let it go. You glance up and see the pall-bearers marching the aisle, their feet like synchronized pendulums swinging their legs onwards. They reach the head of the altar and rest the coffin on its stand, and you make sure not to look directly at the coffin but just above it, where a wreath of lilies has been laid. Your grandmother painted a bouquet of lilies once for your mother's birthday: big, creamy lilies lightly speckled with brown spots, they reminded you of a frothy coffee dusted with chocolate. As the pall-bearers walk back down to the pews, you register the polished box beneath the flowers, and you realise the organ has stopped playing. The vicar requests that you please be seated. The vicar's white robes look as silky as the lily petals in your grandmother's painting. You try to listen to him but you're starting to panic about having to stand up and speak to the church. You take one more look at the coffin. How private it is; how impersonal it is. Can you really be saying goodbye to Grandma if she can't possibly hear your goodbyes through this coffin?

The coffin's not so much to keep the body inside safe, you think; it's to keep it trapped, concealed. There is some comfort in thinking that the body is just a substitute for the real living person that once took you by both hands and launched you from a warm paddling pool on a summer afternoon. After all, it's much easier to say goodbye to the wooden box rather than face the reality that you will never see your grandma again, touch her again, smell lavender and roast beef and talcum powder in her embrace. You cry and the scene around you blurs like wet paint brushed onto a canvas board. You wipe your hand over your eyes, leaving a trail of black mascara on your fingers (you only wore mascara to look more adult), and you look up to where the vicar is giving rehearsed phrases of comfort and protection to 'our sister Sheila.' Soon, you will be expected to do the same.

You look back at your speech which is now blotted with tears. The biro runs into them, outlines them like blue and white acrylic paint merging on a palette. You rub the paper between your fingers, feeling the flat spaces in between the ridges and bumps. You want to believe you'll see Grandma again in heaven — which is what your sister believes — but you can see the evidence of what happens after death right here in this church. Imagine being inside a coffin: trapped in the dark, unable to see or breathe properly, the lid bumping the tip of your nose and toes.

The paper in your hands is quivering so much that you nearly drop it on the floor. You clutch it to your lap, and as you lean forward you see, stitched on a cushion under the bench in front, a picture of the world. You try to calm yourself by concentrating on the cushion's detailed needlework, and you pull your jacket tight around your shoulders and shift from one buttock to the other; you've just noticed a cool breeze tickling your ankles.

A cough and a sob behind you. Your father must have hugged your sister because you hear a rustle of his jacket over your right shoulder.

The vicar says your name and you look up again at the stand. You stand up. You nearly trip on the steps of the altar because you keep looking at the stand to distract you from what's just in front of you.

The stand is shaped like an eagle, its beak smooth and tailored to a point. It's made from a different kind of polished wood. It makes you think of a great bald-headed eagle flying across red and orange canyons, making use of its vast wing span and gliding as smoothly as a crisp paper aeroplane carried by the wind.

But eagles catch their prey and kill it! God, they murder nearly every day just to eat and stay alive; they don't worry about death because it's an everyday occurrence with them. They just carry on flying across oceans and deserts; they keep flying because it's the only thing they know. And when they die they won't be buried. What happens to eagles when they die? In your head you picture an eagle lying on its back in a sandy desert, its wings spread like a newspaper dropped as litter on the street. No-one mourns its death. There's no coffin, no service, no words of comfort or farewell. The plains just carry on as normal, leave the ants to eat away at the decaying body.

One wood is dark, cold and unfamiliar, highly polished and impersonal. The other is honey coloured, dull but not so dull that it's boring to look at; the ridges and bumps of the eagle's feathery torso enable you to step up behind its spread wings, place a hand on either wing, lay down your piece of paper and look out into the faces lining the pews.

Breathe.

Look down, look up, look out.

Sunday / *Jessica Searle*

It's one of those modern churches: a big hall with pink cushioned chairs and an IKEA-style representation of the crucifixion. But the music's good. And the people. Jen goes there for the music and the people.

'Jen, it's so good to see you. God Bless.' Richard embraces her.

'You too, Richard. How's Sue? Valerie tells me she had a fall?'

Richard gives her an update before wishing her a good service, *full of things that the Lord has planned for you.* Jen acknowledges this with a smile, and heads down the corridor to face the rest of the congregation.

Valerie, her favourite 'sister,' beckons Jen over by enthusiastically patting the space next to her. She's sitting on the sofa outside the Ladies, wearing a purple dress suit with a green scarf, hair curled in tight ringlets. Jen's smile becomes more genuine.

'Valerie, my lovely. Are you well?'

'Must you always ask that, my dear?' She tries to tickle Jen as she sits down.

'You know me – always one for good etiquette.'

Valerie laughs, even though it's the same joke as last week. 'Now, come on my child, what is it you really want to know?' She leans forward, waiting for the answer that Jen always gives.

'What's the gossip?'

'Well, Rachel's sister, Jean, broke her other hip on Wednesday. This means that Rachel's been working double time to look after her. I mean, one hip is bad, but two... well... I wouldn't want to be in her shoes. Rachel's clothes don't match today, and her hair isn't properly curled, but I wouldn't mention it. She's trying her best, so leave her be.'

Valerie tells Jen that one of the elders still has cancer, Heather's birthday is on Tuesday (the one that chops the carrots at lighthouse lunches), and Pastor Mark is leaving for Mozambique tomorrow. This is everything she needs to know to get through the half hour of socialising before the service starts.

Back in the car, Jen lets her face relax. Normally she leaves feeling guilt-ridden, but Pastor Mark was preoccupied: the usual *you must give yourself to the Lord* message was absent.

She's got the congregation convinced that she's one of them. Because they believe her, she believes herself.

She fastens her seatbelt, turns the key, winds the window down, and heads for the pub. She sings Eva Cassidy's 'Fields of Gold' as she blurs the hedgerows.

'The usual, Jen?'

'Please, Don.' Donna runs to the kitchen, orders Jen's small roast beef and fruit salad, and then returns to pour her a glass of water.

'So, how was church?'

'It was good. Really good.'

Five minutes later, Jen's Sunday lads turn up.

'Alright lads… how's the week been? Anything new?' Jen puts a twenty on the bar; it's her round. She likes to think this earns her respect.

'Parsons got a new motorbike,' says Cainser.

'Another one?' says Jen. 'What's that now? Seven?'

'Eight…. but it's a Ducati 916.'

'Say no more.'

'See lads. Told you she'd be on my side.' Parsons taps Jen's glass with his.

'It's just cause she fancies you.' The lads cheer and wolf whistle. Jen gives Cainser a friendly thump on the arm.

'Grow up, Cainser. There are better men out there than Parsons… no offence, mate.'

'None taken,' says Parsons, turning red.

Before Cainser has the chance to rib him some more, Jen's food turns up, and the lads fight over footing her bill. Jen eats her meal in the snug, vegetables first. Donna replaces her empty plate with a fruit salad. Jen wishes she'd ordered the cheesecake. Once she finishes, she doesn't go back to the lads. Instead, she sits and listens – she prefers it this way.

Later, Jen follows Nick out to the smoking shelter, and they sit next to each other on one of the picnic benches. She watches him prepare a fag. Before he's finished rolling, he passes it to her. She licks it, seals it, and gives it back.

'I still don't understand why you smoke those things. You don't even fill them properly.'

As he puts the fag in his mouth, he nudges her with his knee. She picks up his lighter, struggles twice before achieving a flame, and his hands cup hers as he inhales. She tries not to breathe: it's not unpleasant, but she doesn't want to let on that she likes it.

'How's Tina?' Asking this question makes her feel good. She's just sitting next to him on a bench, being a friend.

'I've left her at home cleaning the windows.'

'You're a lucky man.'

'I know.' He takes another drag of his cigarette, and seems to move closer, but she could be imagining it.

When she shivers, he puts his arm around her and rubs her shoulder. 'Oh, shut it,' he says, seeing her expression. 'I'm just trying to warm you up. A proper gent.'

'In that case, thank you kindly, sir.' He winks. He laughs. He nudges her. He takes another drag. She breathes.

When Jen next enters the beer garden, having played hand after hand of dominoes, the sun has slumped behind the willow trees, but Nick is unmoved, as if smoking the same cigarette.

'She finally returns,' he says.

Jen takes her place next to him on the bench and rests her head on his shoulder. They sit in smoky silence. Jen knows he's testing her patience, waiting for her to break. She watches him lift the cigarette to his mouth. Before he gets a chance to inhale, Jen snatches it, and threatens to put it out.

'Okay, okay.' Nick raises his hands in surrender. 'Did you win at dommies?'

'Of course.' Jen offers his cigarette back, making him reach across her to get it. 'Pure skill.'

'Half luck.' Instead of retrieving the cigarette, Nick places it in Jen's hand, slotting it between her middle finger and index finger – ready to smoke.

'Are you trying to get me addicted?' she says.

'No. It's just, at my age, lifting a fag requires too much effort.'

'You lazy git.' Jen holds the cigarette to his lips, and he rests his hand round her wrist, stroking her palm with his thumb as he inhales. She closes her eyes and waits for the burn of the filtered orange tip to reach her fingers.

Jen stubs it out and stands up. 'I better get going.'

'You spend hours playing dominoes with those old gits, but you only spare me one cigarette. Do you have to leave?' Nick starts to roll another fag.

'You can hardly talk, Mr "I've got to go, the Mrs needs me."'

Nick holds the unsealed cigarette out to her. Jen attempts a sigh that comes out as a laugh. She bends down, lifts his hands to her lips, and licks the cigarette.

'Talking of the Mrs,' says Nick, as he seals the cigarette and puts it in his mouth, 'she rang to say she's staying at Mother-in-law's, so I'm free.'

'You'll be here later?'

'Stupid question. Now run along, you religious nut. Twice in one day… I'll never understand that. Hope they don't make you feel guilty for sitting there and thinking about me the whole time.'

Jen makes her way to Valerie, who's waiting for her on the same sofa outside the Ladies. If it wasn't for her change of clothes, Jen could imagine her sitting there all day, waiting to pass on the next piece of gossip.

'You missed a right old scene this morning, Jen. You know Heather, the one that chops and peels the carrots for Lighthouse lunches? Well, she's received complaints. For the past five years, she's been chopping the carrots into circles, but at the last lunch, she cut them into strips. You wouldn't believe the uproar, Jen. Just terrible. The Pastor's wife confronted her in the Ladies. Broke into tears, the poor thing.'

The band starts to play, so Jen gets up, offers Valerie a hand, and they walk into the worship hall arm in arm.

This time, Pastor Mark's in full flow. His Bible is open on the lectern, but this makes no sense to Jen; he always recites the scriptures from memory. Jen suspects that it's something to do with tradition. They've already got the IKEA cross and padded chairs; leaving the Bible behind for the Sermon might be one step too far.

'For some reason,' he says, 'he could not feel the Holy Spirit. For some reason, God's Holy Ghost had left him, and the thrill was gone.'

Jen looks round at the congregation. Some of them are on their feet with their arms raised. Some of them are kneeling, hands resting on their laps, palms facing up. The rest look peaceful and somewhere else – their eyes are closed, their breathing's steady, and they're swaying to some hidden beat. Some say Amen. Some say Hallelujah. Some say Praise the Lord. Jen is sitting with her legs crossed. If they look at her, they'll see that she's never had that thrill.

'Every child oughta have that feeling, when you come to know God, and have God down in the crevices of your soul. Well, a lotta of you in here have come the same way… just like David.'

At this point the Pastor pauses and the echoers join in. They repeat 'just like David' in unison.

'Every time you hear the band sing, you clap and you dance, but you've lost your soul. Every time you hear the Elders pray, you hold out your hands, but you don't feel a thing.'

'You don't feel a thing.' The echoes grow stronger.

Jen looks round again at the kneeling, raising, swaying congregation. Somebody puts a hand on her shoulder.

'I am telling you, there are people in this room today that have lost, or never found, the love that our beautiful Lord has for us.'

The hand on her shoulder squeezes. Jen feels like the Pastor's talking to her. He knows. He sees her sitting there with crossed legs and he knows.

'"For God so loved the world, that he gave his one and only Son, that whoever believes in him shall not perish but have eternal life."'

The strangest thing is that she wants His love. She knows, deep down, it's the reason she's here. She wipes her forehead with the back of her arm. She's sweating, and hopes no one notices.

'He gave his Son's life so that we could live.'

Jen wants to raise her hands and say Amen, but she doesn't.

'For those of you who feel like David, I ask you to do a brave thing. Stand up. Stand up and we'll pray for you. We'll welcome you in. The Lord, our God, will wake you up.'

There's something about the room, and the voices, and the people. She shivers. Her hands go numb. Whatever it is, it's enough. She stands up.

It's eight pm. Jen is sitting in the beer garden, head on Nick's shoulder, waiting for the quiz to start. She hasn't told him what happened at church. He'd laugh it off as a joke, and say it was a ruse to cover up what she was really doing – thinking of him.

Jen lets his words blur and looks round at the beer garden in the lamplight.

Steve is sitting with Born and Bred, trying to keep up with their tennis game of gibberish – 'Did you 'ear 'bout ole' Willy Wombul? Chu'd hisself under a bus down

Nanny Noony Lane.'

Parsons and Cainser are in the corner, talking motorbikes and sharing jokes – 'Why did the Polish man cross the road? Cause he stole the chicken's job.'

Metal garden chairs, painted white, with cushions for comfort, sit around the matching metal table. According to Born and Bred, the table and chairs have been in 'exac' same place fur six'y yur'. Everyone thinks they're making it up, but Jen believes them. The creepers climb the wrought-iron-meshed fence, round the chair legs, in and out of the chair backs, and through the chair arms. Jen likes to think that if she sits here long enough, the creepers will welcome her in, shaking her hand.

Nick's ready for another cigarette and Jen's got his lighter. She gets a flame first time and ignores his mocking praise.

Jen loves the view from this chair. The whole garden glows at her: symmetrical pathways and grass patches join with flowers and statues that meet at a large stone barbecue. The chef turns spiced sausages and burgers. Boules thump on gravel. The chef's dog runs back and forth, thinking it's a game of fetch. Jen listens to the crackle of the fire and stares into the flames.

After a moment, some kids run up to her with empty crisp packets. She sits and admires their awed faces as they stare at her hands. Their eyes try to keep up with her fingers as she presents each of them with a neatly folded triangle.

The bell rings – time for the quiz.

'You ready?' says Nick.

'Bring it.'

Nick gets up and offers Jen his hand. She takes it, and they stand there, arms linked, breathing in the smoke and spiced sausages. Nick drops his cigarette in front of her. She puts it out with a twist of her foot, and they walk into the pub, arm in arm.

'Second's not bad, considering the amount I've had to drink,' says Nick.

'And my terrible general knowledge,' says Jen.

'Yeah, you're pretty stupid for a clever girl.'

They're sitting outside Nick's house in Jen's car. One of the rare times that Nick isn't smoking.

'Tina's done a good job on those windows,' says Jen.

'Yeah, she's good like that.'

Jen watches Nick's loose tobacco strands fall to the footwell as he taps the air with a ready-rolled cigarette.

'You coming in?' he says.

'What? To read you a bedtime story?'

They laugh, and Nick wraps his arms round her. Fosters and cigarettes mask the smell of Tina's perfume that clings to his clothes. He places a kiss on Jen's forehead, and another on her neck, before letting her go. He hesitates for a moment, looks at something in the mirror, and then, with the heaviness of adult movement, he opens the passenger door. 'Now, young lady, drive safe. I know what you women are like – bloody useless.'

Once the door is closed, Jen turns the CD player on, and Nick lights his cigarette. As she does a three-point-turn, Glen Campbell's 'Rhinestone Cowboy' fades out, and Matt Redman's 'Blessed Be Your Name' begins. The song reminds her of church. As she drives off, she forgets to wave goodbye.

She ignores the guitar and drums and listens to the words. By the end of the song, she's home. She goes to play it again, but Malcolm jumps onto the bonnet and starts to meow — they must've locked the cat flap.

Jen gets out of the car, and heads inside with Malcolm on her heels. She lets him into the kitchen and fills his biscuit bowl. As she's about to go upstairs, she notices a post-it note on the table:

> Hi Jen love. Hope you've had a
> good day. Leftovers in the
> fridge if you want them.
> Big hugs. Mum xXx

Jen opens the fridge. Roast potatoes or fruit salad. She stands with the fridge door open, trying to decide.

The Cool Generation / *Joshua Simpson*

Chill   Cold

     passive

                          Nippy

     Unenthusiastic   Lukewarm

Tepid   Indifferent

     Apathetic   Half-hearted

Distant   Remote

    Unfriendly   Aloof

                         Unwelcoming

    Frosty

THE COOL GENERATION
AN EXTRACT

Offhand

    Unresponsive

                       Stand-offish

   Uncommunicative   Undemonstrative

                 Self-controlled

Calm

    Composed

                Unperturbed

            Unmoved Unmovable

    Laid-back   With it   Up to the minute

        Moderated   Unintense

    Unmotivated   Emotionless

Foreword

I'm so cool.

Her Fingernail

I looked out the front window that framed Colchester town:

[
A lullaby scene of tall dark buildings shedding ice. Snow slips from rooftops in wedges. White Adam's apples slide along the throats of drainpipes, gulping. Snowflakes parachute.
]

I was at Twisters, leaning on the bar, when a fingernail woodpecked my lumbar. I turned.
- Hey, you're Blank, right? (I recognized the girl from my estate and college. She pushed her face forwards, eyebrows raised, smiling.) As if you're here! That's so weird. (It wasn't.) You live around the corner from me, don't you? Your name's Blank, right?

She was Hispanic, callipygian, but she didn't impress me, and I wasn't attracted to her (I was).
- Yeah, it is, and... I do know you, you know? I mean. I can't... ha–
- I'm Gaby. Gabriella.
- Yes, I knew it, that's the one. You go to Sixth Form, right?

I ordered us each a G & T. We watched the bar like a tropical aquarium:

Quick-small	bartenders	in	hawaiian	shirts		
darted	behind	fridge	doors,	under	taps,	into
drawers,	like	fish.	It	was	^h_eT$_i$c.	A
girl	in	green	sequins	flits	between	two	red
shirts,	dashes	under	the	arms	of	her
supervisor,	picks	two	bottles	of	rosé
from	the	bottom	shelf	and,	arcing	around
an	open	drawer,	dives	under	a	bottleopener
mid-flight	and	zips	back	up	to	the	bar.
Each	movement	was	*spaz-mod-dik,*	but	no	fish
collided.						

We talked for five minutes. In retrospect, I notice the tells I didn't care to see:
1. Her over-enthusiastic smiling
2. Hands on my shoulders/chest
3. Sorting her breasts/dress
4. Leaning in to me
5. Locked eye contact

The encounter ended like this: she jabbed me in the sternum with an acrylic nail and said:
– I'm driving into college Monday. Do you want a lift?
– That would be great, save me jumping on the bus.
I was just being polite; I wasn't interested (I was). She put her number in my phone. She put it in my phone. I didn't take it from her. She put it in *my* phone. I made sure that was clear to all who enquired.

Her Car

Sunday morning, 10.20am, I scrolled through missed calls and unread SMS in bed. I remembered Gaby. I scrolled through contacts down to G. There she was. Pfft. I curled back into my blankets and spiralled into sleep. She was nothing special. (I dreamed her faceprint into my pillow.)

I didn't text Gaby until I had to:

Hey, is this Gaby's Taxi Service? :P What time you leaving in morning? I do not want to get on the peasant wagon if I can help it! Lol. Blank X	Six minutes later.	Heeey, yes it is! :P Oh god I was so drunk last nyt. I bet you thought, oh god who is this scary drunk woman? lol. I'm leaving at 8.45, that cool? X

When my Monday alarm rang at 7 a.m. I sprang from my bed as if I had been poised in starting blocks. I showered, shaved, shat, dressed, ate Weetabix, pissed, drank a pint of tea, brushed teeth, then hair, sprayed deodorant, then aftershave, styled my hair into a quirky quiff, pulled on my brown leather coat, slipped my hands into gloves, and sprung out the door *into italic snowfall.*

I checked my watch the whole way. 8.40 a.m., 8.41 a.m., 8.42 a.m.. Would she leave without me if I were late? What if her watch is fast? What if mine is slow? Pfft, I don't want her lift anyway, just would've been better than waiting for the bus in the snow (I told myself).

I found her parked around the next corner, engine warmly beating, smiling through the dead skin of frost on the windscreen. I opened the door, jumped inside – warmth – and shut it quick.

– Hey, are we late?
– No, it's only just 8.45. You didn't rush to get here did you?
– Pfft, no.

We crept out of Pertwee Drive, trenching the axle-high snow. From a T-junction we nudged onto the main road. The tarmac there was gritted: three black slush-lines running either side of wheel tracks. Tanks had driven along this road. Reaching Colchester town, I noticed Gaby was taking the route along Southway and over St Botolph's roundabout. The bus route. You could remove ten minutes by turning off before Southway and driving up Balkerne hill. I didn't mention it. She must've been taking this route for nearly two years. No need to embarrass her. I rode into college with Gaby all week.

Friday morning, we crawled out of the village, rushed down the main road, and interlaced through the town centre. I had decided not to tell her about the shortcut. It was relaxing to spend thirty minutes listening to Arctic Monkeys in a warm car before class (and inhaling mouthfuls of peppermint and aspartame every time she exhaled; gum snapped in her mouth at every consonant). That's all it was.

Her Eyeball

Saturday night, Paul, Owen and I were back at Twisters. I watched the melee of transactions over the bar. There is never any physical contact: notes held at corners are plucked away; coins are dropped from overturned hand into upturned hand; cash is placed on the bar.

Owen, seeing over my shoulder, informed me that Gaby had entered. A menagerie of giggles close behind me. She came to the bar, to my immediate left, ordered a couple of Alcopops – lipstick red and neon blue – and plugged the red one to her lips. From side-on I watched her head tilt back, the red bottle glugging. Her eyeballs were not round, I realised. The irises were the shapes of blisters. Bubble-wrap bubbles. Domes. (Now I realize that all eyes are like this, but it took hers to show me; next time you look at someone, look at an eyeball from the side.)

Please do not attach any emotional meaning to this. It's just something I noticed.

A few drinks later I got up and headed for the toilet. Drunk, it felt wobbly, low gravity, amusing to walk. I moved into the back room where the band was playing. I noticed the rustic wooden pillars standing far from one another:][people][dancing][between][them][. If they were to stand together they'd become weaker; the roof would collapse onto them: this would not do. I noticed the indie band's guitars, the strings running parallel, a trench of silence between each string. If one string was too close to another, touching even, it would ruin both their sounds, smother and rape the harmony.

I slouched through the archway and down the corridor. Here, two doors face each other: on one there is painted a little white man; on the other a little white woman. Pulled open at the same time, the little white man and woman look as if they're going to touch. As they get close they glide past one another, a four millimetre gap between them.

Returning back through the archway, I saw, at the corner table, Gaby with her fingernail on an Indian boy's chest. What did I care? I turned around to the bar. People, like fish, moved in rich, colourful bursts. They all danced and dodged at once. But they were slipping past one another, never touching.

Under snow, I waited for a taxi. <u>Her Fingernail</u> prodded the back of my neck.

—   I've not drunk much; do you want a lift back?

She put away <u>Her Phone</u>, gestured towards <u>Her Car</u>,

—   That would be cool, yeah.

(I stared at <u>Her Eyeball</u> from the side, and kept my shortcuts secret, prolonging my time in the warmth.)

On Pretending I Want A One Night Stand While Actually Wanting Love But Not Declaring It As She Walks Out The Door

Slam,

Sigh,

Sigh

Two Ships at Sea

On their backs in a cart at the back of a freight train, the hard pulse from the locomotive sifts sawdust from stacked slats of timber, dusting them the way that, when on the beach, sand falls through your fingers as you look out to sea.

'I can tell you something about ships,' he said.

'Please tell me something about ships,' she said.

'The interesting thing about ships,' he said, 'is that when there's two ships both at anchor, in proximity in a calm sea, they tend to slowly drift together.'

Sand shuffles and spills through the timber.

'Because of the wind blowing, and that?'

'No,' he said, 'not that. Each ship shields the neighbouring vessel from lateral waves on one side; so, by small increments, outside forces will marry them side by side.'

'You think we'll be pushed together?'

'Something like that,' he said.

They rocked as the cart hit a curve and the girl bumped the back of her head. 'So, if we do nothing, what happens? We just get closer and closer?'

'Yes,' said the boy, back embattled as the floor kicked and rattled again.

The girl cleared the dust from her windpipe. 'This thing with the ships happens quickly?'

'At first it's quite slow; then it's quick.'

That stuff with the boats, thought the young girl, I hope it's not all about ships.

Mamihlapinatapai[14] (I)

Luke exited the office of AT&T Cell Phones and walked into the lobby with a book, *The Cool Generation* by Josh Simpson, under his arm. The book jacket was white with words scattered about and 'The Cool Generation' printed bold across it. The author, obviously modest and probably handsome, had left his name off the front. Carla entered, sat in a chair opposite, hunched forth, elbow deep in her handbag, withdrew a book, pushed her shoulders back into the seat, crossed one leg over the other and planted the book upright on her knee. Luke read 'The Cool Generation' on the cover of her book.

This is what he noticed first.

Second, he noticed the reader; he saw black hair, white face, black scarf, white blouse, black trousers, white socks, black pumps – a chameleon napping on a chessboard. Carla was ectomorph with an elven face: a thin straight philtrum, ears poking through her hair, fine angular eyebrows. Distracted, Luke collapsed his book; he could read no more. He started reading the room. The clock face said 12.04, the calendar said SEP / 10th, the women's book-cover said 'frosty,' 'detached,' 'indifferent.' He started to read his book again, but not from his copy; he was reading the book from the reflection in her face now. People started to filter in from lunch breaks. When she stopped reading, clapped the book, and untangled her legs, Carla caught Luke staring, reading her.

'Sorry. You won't believe what a coincidence this is.' He held up his book.

'Oh. Wow. This is pretty damn random. I've never seen anyone else with this book 'till now.'

They talked. They laughed. Carla got up and sat next to Luke to compare books. They talked about the book. They laughed. They talked about *books*. They laughed. They talked about art. They talked about reality. They laughed. They promised to meet again once they had finished the final story of *The Cool Generation*. Luke's hand jumped to his thigh and pressed down flat: a roof to muffle his ringtone.

'Sorry.' He checked his cell. 'Wow, I really need to get back to work. I'm pretty late.'

'Oh dear.' She stood with him. 'I best be off too.'

'So...' said Luke.

'Well...' said Carla

Neither of them wanted to leave.

'Hm.'

'Enjoy the book.'

'You too.'

'Okay then.'

'Okay... bye,' said Luke

---

14   Yaghan term. Definition: A look shared by two people, both wishing the other will offer something they both desire, but are unwilling to do themselves (often due to personal, situational or societal pressures).

'See ya later,' said Carla

'Take care,' said Luke.

'You too,' said Carla.

Both: 'See ya round, maybe.'

Both: 'Jinx!'

Neither of them had moved.

They were standing facing one another despite exhausting phatics. Luke held his cell in his right hand in front of him. Carla held hers in her right hand in front of her. They both held their books, behind them, in their left.

I'll see her around another time, he thought.

I'll see him around soon, she thought.

Obeying their jinx, they unstuck from each other, back to work, another day in the World Trade Center.

Mamihlapinatapai (II)

On September the eleventh Luke awoke at 4.15am with a migraine. He swallowed aspirin and sparkling water. He lay in bed awake until 7am. He swallowed more aspirin and sparkling water. He phoned AT&T to let them know he wasn't coming in. He swallowed more aspirin and sparkling water. He turned off the lights and TV, and he drew the curtains. He tuned the radio to Classic FM and hugged his bed sheets all day.

On September the eleventh Carla awoke to a cold apartment. She cocooned her dressing gown over her pyjamas and waddled to the boiler in the kitchen. Her thermal socks and coat-tails of cotton became soaked as she stepped into the kitchen. The entire tile surface was flooded from the boiler. She called her plumber before calling AT&T and letting them know she was going to be late.

On September the eleventh two 767-223ER aircrafts bombed into the World Trade Center as Luke lay on his bed and Carla wrung pyjama pants over the bathroom sink.

Luke forgot about Carla, Carla forgot about Luke. They did this actively: they had to hide their copies of *The Cool Generation*; they had to distract themselves and put it out of their minds. But every time they saw the image of those smoking towers on TV, one would think about the other and feel like one of those towers. For two years neither of them ever read that final story.

Luke still thinks of Carla, Carla still thinks of Luke.

One Saturday in December 2003, they both entered the Christmas market on 9th Avenue from opposite ends. As they drew intersecting paths in the snow towards the centre, they came to the equidistant food court. Across families hunched in circles biting steaming turkey burgers they saw each other. They both, for a moment, felt they were looking at the person they met and fell in love with twenty-six months ago. They both paused, reading one another, cogitating. Then fearful that they might have the wrong person, or worse that it was the right person but they no longer reciprocated the love, or worse still that they never reciprocated the love and the love was imagined, they shook their heads, walked away, keeping their cool but feeling cold.

Taking My Pulse

When a flame is touched to a point on the circumference of a gas-ring hob, it ignites the halo of gas. If you watch carefully, though, you'll see this is not instant. The fire starts at the point of collision and spreads in two semi-circular arcs which meet at the other side of the ring.

The blood tunnelling down her vein, behind the crêpe paper skin of her rasceta, was an encroaching flame. It touched the tip of my fingerprint before spreading around its circumference in two arcs to meet at the other side.

Then the next pulse – pulse – pulse – pulse – pulse bumps my finger like a steam train passenger.

As I lay my middle finger beside my forefinger on her wrist, like a knackered husband falling into bed alongside his wife, she slid her supinated fingers under my downturned hand and pressed two digits on the underside of my veins.

When I remember this moment I think of M.C. Escher's 'Drawing Hands.' Those two pencil-drawn hands, each drawing one another, being the artist and the art of the other, interdependent, eternally paired.

I think of the double-helix structure of DNA, a twisted ladder.

I think of our yin-yang fridge magnet.

I think of Velcro.

I choose not to remember her two fingers withdrawing like a pair of snail's eyestalks. I do not recall her saying, 'I can't feel anything.'

Poetry

And Doubts Leave, Following Him

she drops the mirror
> and realigns
> to pull in her full face
> nailing it to today's date

> > *white rabbits pinch and punch*
> > *the translucence of her senses,*
> > *scratching like diamond on glass nerves*

> she watches her lips
> twitching the after effect
> of the sound quake
> that yesterday, killed cupids
> with their own arrows

> > *they fell Satan-like to ground*

> and sees her eyes,
> aridly staring at the hole
> in her heart, drawn
> but not quartered

> and feels her shoulders
> drop a notch

> > *lowering*
> > *like her eye-line*

> her spine
> ratchet skywards

> *raised*
> *like expectations*

> tasting the sweetness
> of the dust of the day

Dawn

She kneels beneath the coloured glass
of the man with the lamb in his arms,
aware of the glare concealing his face.

She spits to polish the oak feet
of the stand of the flat backed bird,
then moves to the brass of its outstretched wings...

When its shine burns her eyes
she stops, calling for shadows
from dark corners, the softness of day light

to filter through the brick-blocked windows
and fan its fabled *medieval* colours -
and put the pew-length lighting strip to shame.

I Want

to travel a path less linear
than the allotted slot of birth to death.

to master the knack of hitching a ride
on the past of another's time,

ignoring the pointlessness of incognito.

to look in the face of a sepia-ed photo
and know its colour, its full dimension.

to slide back and forth and compare the truths
of then with current conjectures.

to whisper in your ear
Go see a doctor

to be your daughter again.

Emma Potter

Answer your Phone

When you took her call,
how were you to know
that he was dying in the next room?
While you shouted down the phone
about charred pizza and late bed times
and inappropriate television,
he was sitting by the wall
with a red plastic spade,
prying at the plug socket.
His screams were squelched
under electric zing and her voice
bellowing in your ear.

You find him with his fingers splayed,
spade abandoned by the plug,
soft little body, eyes still open;
you think it's a game.
You scoop him up and his head falls
like when you carry him from the sofa.
When you took her call –
she complained that you never answer –
how were you to know the glue
would come unstuck?
That his tiny fingertips
fit perfectly in the gaps?

AWOL

Out by the boats he's coiling ropes,
sealing cracks with clay
and new wood, using old bits of string
to mend nets; he scrubs at their decks.

The sun high at noon,
heels hitting boards, he swings his legs
off the side of the dock, picks at bread
and swallows without complaint,

without a thought to the gaps in the ranks;
'Sam Meadows' is left unanswered.
counting numbers and learning words
won't make him a living.

When the sun rolls low, the officer swings
by the shadows of cabins,
a short breath in the dark
Sam Meadows hides.

C.V: Mark Brampton

Malmore Maternity Ward 1952:
> -Three weeks premature, two weeks intensive care.

Two years of crying sleeping eating, talking walking falling.

Three years of Balmore Daycare:
> -Tricycles, sun-naps, story-times, chicken-pox.

One year of Rannoch Reception:
> -Apple juice, A – Z, holding hands.

Ten years of Rannoch Primary/Rannoch State:
> -First kiss: Year six disco, Emily Tummel, behind the cafeteria, spilt
> lemonade.
> -First real kiss: Sinead, a gypsy, Dalwhinnie Forest school trip, Sugar
> Maple.

-First sexual experience:
> -Catherine, a floor supervisor at a chocolate factory, fruit and nut
> department, parent's bed.

-First fight:
> -Green Panther toilets, Guy Brutchell, blood on the tap, three dentist
> appointments.

-First good sexual experience:
> -Sinead, Edinburgh City Library, contemporary fiction.

Two years of Edinburgh South College:
> -First relationship: Emily Tummel, candles on the beach, Saturday night
> takeaways
> and half watched films.
> -First drugs: 2/3 of a spliff, L.S.D, basement flat, Roxy Music's first album,
> If There Is Something.
> -Four months of parent's money, cycling to the cinema, leaning on pool
> cues eating pistachio nuts, afternoon sex, arcades, C.V workshops.

First job:

-Cleaning the cabins of long-distance airplanes, soggy sick bags, bomb scares.

First marriage:

-Emily Tummel, hand-stitched invitations, Greenside Parish Church, four tiered cake, family Bentley, Maldives, bill sent to bride's father.

Second job:

-Advertising department of a chocolate factory, copywriting, under-qualified.

First affair:

-Catherine, Christmas party, nibbles, against the desk, job requirement.

First divorce:

-Black Mount Court, swift, efficient, brutal.

First rebound:

-Sinead, Black Mount Cove, drinking in the surf, swam too far, brought back with the morning catch.

All right Grammar, alright?

It begins with a prefix (anti, pseudo, mis)
ends happily with a suffix (ism, fy, ly,)
(Anti-Americanism)

Blame Iron Age India who had the definitive
to stop splitting up their infinitive.
(To boldly go where no language had gone)

Never use a big word to avoid a little;
your text will become tremendously noncommittal.
(They were so full of lasciviousness that they couldn't leave the house)

Remember the farther you go the further you get,
and if you've hanged something it's by their neck.
(You may have hung the painting, and hanged the painter)

Don't end your sentences with a preposition,
or dangle your modifiers in an unfavourable position.
(I once wrestled a bear dressed as a cheerleader. I wanted to know why)

The tautologist phrases of long-winded verbosity,
is the English language taken to excess.
(The small green garden cress was sadly deeply troubled)

Watch your repetition: closely scrutinise accidental mistakes
so it's the honest truth, the truth and nothing but the truth.
(Harold was murdered and killed by a murderer who killed him)

Oh and always (whoa! Interjection) end with a punch.

Crow Country

we travel West Northwest
                leaving the city
                    by the back door
            we hurtle through the flatness
follow the landscape of the Midlands
                    the history under acres
                        of miles of grassy roads
we slip our cargo station by station
        reach the crossing place
the backside of the country
now dolmens
        and drumlins
                ringforts
        and burial chambers
to where the Queen of Crow Country
is buried upright facing her enemies

Rock

In the cliff face I saw a yours.

As familiar as my own,
I wanted to reach out and stroke it
until the stone melted
liquefying under my touch,
I wanted to knead and caress until
your features re-arranged themselves
and were exactly how I remembered,
I wanted to touch your smile once more;
feel it under my fingers
and trace your softened rock features.
I wanted to pull you from the fissure,
sculpting my deep memory of you
from the moleskin-covered shoreline
to have you born to me again
– to shatter the flint in me.

Island

the sand skims the beach
                of the shifting tide
like a crawling shiver of long ripples
                    moving pebbles
are smocked by ebb and flow
       sand pock-marked by driving rain
in this parish   my universe
        you sit
        poised
      and snake-like
    in the drift of my dream
you still me   and bind me
     with tongue flicks

   as you shed with ease
my skin is ripped from my flesh
        by your shocking touch

Seed

An entire summer sits
dry and wrinkled in my palm.
I hide it in the soil
like a secret thought.
It swells in moist darkness,
grips earth with white roots.
It sends a pale emissary
to find a path to the sun
tunnelling upwards
through the crust,
pulling the world with it.

Last Train

A fluorescent tube in the station office
flickers an incoherent warning.
Leaves mutter in the breeze,
shatters the street lamps' glow
above the oily puddles on the tarmac
where an empty car waits
engine idling.
On the other side of the railings
a plastic bag
tumbles down the track like a lost soul.

Six O'clock

I edge between snoozing cars and cross the bridge.
A cat sits on the track below, eyes half closed,
ready to dodge the six-twenty to Bristol Parkway.
The smell of baking bread tugs at my senses;
the sun yawns and stretches its rays behind me.
A robin follows me along the fence, flies
past my face. A dog barks from a bush;
its elderly owner whistles from Eileen's park bench.
I reach the abandoned swimming pool
used to store sea-front construction materials;
Save our Tropicana posters litter the promenade lampposts.

I tread around limpets living on the salt-eroded wooden steps
and watch the dust float as I thud onto the sand;
it sneaks into my trainers and grinds under my feet.
I follow the grooves of other peoples' footsteps
to avoid sinking my own into the mustard-coloured grains.
My iPod shuffles to Maroon Five's *Harder to Breathe*
as I jog towards the sodden tide-line. Mini puddles start to swell
around each step, sand specks flick at the white leather.
I dodge the dripping water and pass through the pier's girders.
I jump over a crumbling sailboat dug into the wet sand
by a little girl's daddy with a forgotten pink spade.

Naomi Wilson

Another Summer's Day

The blanket is a patchwork pattern
of reassuring memory. I lie on it,
close my eyes to the sun's kaleidoscopic shapes
and the wind breathes out your laugh.

It is too bright to make shapes
out of clouds. So I roll onto my stomach
make daisy chains and lambs' tails
brushing the petals against my lips.

I packed plums for today but I find them
burst at the bottom of my bag — slime over
my cling-filmed sandwiches. The last time
we laughed and made plum pudding.

But this time they're ruined —
squashed from the weight
of my water bottle. You always said cartons
were best for picnics.

The Gift.

One liquorice night you call me.
I stick my head out of the window
and wait for the photograph of you
to appear on the black road.

I thought I'd wait for you like this.
You're only five minutes away, you said.
I lay my head on the dirt-ridden roof
like a hard cracked pillow

grey paint scraping against my cheek.
My eyes water as the streetlights
fuzz amber everywhere. I stare for you,
refuse to blink in-case I miss you,

and then I begin to imagine what you'll look like.
You walk to my gate
pretending to be self-conscious.
And when you are close enough

I see there are flowers.
I close my window and run
to the stairs, down, then wavering
on the last, near the door.

If I had waited and let you knock
come down with no hesitancies or thoughts
and opened it to you, you would be standing
with the first bunch of daisies in your awkward hands.

Rooftop Kick-ups

His name is José
playing kick-ups on the brick-red
roof of Café Pelé,
his personal record twenty-six.

Among washing hung to dry,
beneath the birds and the kites
in the lee of de Periquita,
t-shirts stained redder than brick.

José's mother
appealed for a burial, received
a ticket on her car for her troubles.
The police did not tell her
they had lost the body,

moved it to another district
to reduce a statistic.
And besides, José's jaw
was all that was left of his head.

Rome

Vespas are motorbikes without the middle bit.
They wurr. They purr.
The 80's ones chuckle
like reminiscing old men
who relish in their right
to puff great black clouds.
Rome
is a city of bad drivers,
most of them, on Vespas.
The cypresses and sweet bays
do their best to give a fresh smell of Italy
to the tourists in their moment
of Facebook glory.

Hegelian Dialect

I am motion,
        changing place, position,
                power of movement.
mocioun, *motion*, *motio*, *motus*, *movere*,
manner of moving, gait, gesture,
           a proposal to a deliberative assembly.
an application made to a court or judge for an order, ruling.
evacuation of the bowels, excrement.
inward prompt, impulse, inclination.
a machination mechanism.
an active operation.
to direct, move, signal
            motioned to her to enter.

I am still,
        motionless,
silent, hushed, tranquil, as water,
           as wine.
stillness, silence, a photograph,
           a distilling apparatus
stiller to drip, *stillre*, *stilla*,
as previously, as yet, in the future as in the past,
           eventually.
even, in addition, nevertheless, quietly,
at or to a greater distance or degree.
to calm,
to hush, allay, appease, subdue, cause to subside,
           to make still,
           to become still.

Luke op den Brouw

Wall

'Maybe a week
maybe longer
they've got the guns
but we've got the numbers[15] '
says the wall in red
and green.
Chips of stone rove
700 kilometres through
olive groves
through
fields and rocky waste
schools and charcoal roads
mosques and dust bowls.
A daughter chokes in a cloud of tear gas
clutching her one-legged doll.
United Nations:
'Where are your treaties
your proclamations now!?'
asks the wall.
The concrete stains
a stench of heat
and acrylic graffiti.
Like a soldier who has
a dove with olive branch tattoo
'I am here to keep the peace'
the slabs stamp into the dirt.
Two faces
the Blue Star of David across his back
and the other:
a voice.
'Fire your bullets … you villain …
for I won't play at murder
or run away
my blood fertilises
and refreshes this land[16] '
says the wall in white
and black.
Eyes watch from high bastions
the rape and murder and loss

15   Graffiti on the Apartheid Wall
16   From Mbarka Mint al-Barra's poem *Message from a Martyr*

Luke op den Brouw

every night men and women cry
each day they turn the dust
of their existence.
A black silhouette of a girl
strives to reach the top
pulled to salvation by balloons.
'*Jidar al-fasl al-'unsuri*'[17]

---

17   Translation: *Racial segregation wall*

Son of the Hunter

He smells
gun oil, eggs, hash browns
and bacon heaved in by the pound.
His Father shouts from the garage
'Five minute shower'
so he cleans all he can manage.

Forest Land Rover to East Grinstead,
passing through the beaten mounds.
The father moves on ahead,
leading the party with the hounds
and all the cars and all the wives left in town,
'There's a change of plans, little savage'
as he takes the beating stick from his hand,
and hands him a double barrel.

The Son stands ten yards abreast,
just like the other men that surround
the bramble nest.
Pheasants erupt from the down-
lands,
he pulls the trigger and the Berretta yawns,
plucking the bird in its hopeful barrage

The brained bird still twitching in the dog's mouth
the Son fails to resist the urge to disgorge
so he cleans all he can manage

When Grandpa Found You

Wonder how it was for Grandpa
when he found you wedged
between the porcelain bathtub
and cold curve of the toilet.

You: waxen and pulse-less
limbs strewn, sporting a sport-sock
tourniquet, the needle standing
straight up like a turkey thermometer.

Your last blink:
the asinine bolt caps —
the ones that always fall off
while cleaning, pressing into linoleum.

Flesh holding sewage down,
like your body
taking in the bad Mexican brown
a final plunge not to be flushed.

The mirror: the only witness
in this sterile silence
as you spiral away like shampoo
circling the drain, joining other
cast offs in subterranean sewage ways.

Wonder how it was for Grandpa,
discovering your big body laid out
in the smallest room in the house:
the dead son of his dead son.

Mr Psychosexual

£100 an hour
to return sensuality
to the self, I don't know why
this makes me think of thick
American pancakes topped
with a nob of butter and dripping
with maple syrup; cooked
an even brown on both sides.
You're the cast iron griddle
for sexual bodywork.

Your services include:
Renewing the Yoni with Intimate Massage
described like a caving expedition
with a bit of an edge; the possibility
of getting stuck, losing your way
or falling from the precipice;
with you – the guiding rope
bringing us both
back to the light.

The testimonials made me want
to sign myself over,
take the leap from an airplane
free-falling in your fingers
flushed as the earth rushes to greet us,
the jolt as we are lifted
suspended in the cosmos…yes,
I'll just sign and print right there,
thank you.

Mary's Labour

I don't buy the miracle
birth business,
having worked at it myself.

Immaculate Conception
it may have been, but there is no way
He bypassed that pelvic gateway.

Did Our Lady scream?
Or perhaps she made animal noises
while the ox and the ass mooed and brayed along.

It's possible she tried to hold it in
like a silent Scientologist
(the sound I mean, not Him.)

Did the Virgin Mother squat
while He slid out,
caught before He hit the desert floor?

Did He cause a Perineal tear with His arrival?
It certainly wouldn't be the last pain
He would cause her.

And what about the blood, the faeces,
all the usual bodily fluids
– the mess on Mary's thighs?

Did Joseph have to bite the umbilical cord
and with one mastication
cut the ties to both mother and Father?

Did she have any trouble passing the placenta?
And when she did, was it wrapped
and preserved – a sacrament or later relic?

But it's more likely angels assisted
celestial midwives gently wiping
the sore and innermost parts

with anointed deistic garments,

touching brow with hallowed hands,
whispering the rapturous truth:

You are a goddess
You are a goddess
You are a goddess.

Prose

The End of All Things / *Duncan Dicks*

This evening the massing of people is around a small river course. It is dry but there may be water beneath. Someone must dig to find water. The digging will be with hands, the sand and mud seeping into the cuts in dry skin, and beneath fingernails. If we find water and it is poisoned then the one who digs will die the way many died before the walk.

Kukua and I hold hands and watch. She reminds me of a blood lily, her head too big for its stalk. I lean close and look in her ear. I waft away the flies but they come back, crowding her lips, her eyes, her nose, her ear. Her ear smells bad. She stares straight ahead into the crowd.

If no-one digs then there will certainly be no water. Soon someone will give in. I can hear them now shouting in whispers because nobody has the energy to argue for long.

It is like listening to a television drama with the sound turned down very low. Mama and Kukua and I used to watch the television in the evenings. Mama made us watch. She said that Papa learned English by listening to the radio so we were lucky to have television. We watched the BBC which Mama said was the most educational. She said that the Queen of England watched the BBC and checked that they spoke properly.

A man is pushed from the crowd, forced to step out onto the riverbed. He shakes his head.

'No. Please, no.' He is crying. A dry crying, but still I see a silvered trail down one cheek. He whispers, his throat unable to carry anything louder. 'Please, walk on. Like Moses we must walk on. We become weak standing here. Tomorrow we will arrive.'

But they crowd around him. A woman pushes forwards, holding a baby. She calls out in the same cracking whisper. 'Where will we arrive? There is nowhere. We are cursed, not chosen like Moses.'

The man who won't dig tries to step around but other people stand beside the woman and demand that he answer.

'We are walking from hell, like the Book of Revelation says, like Moses walked from Egypt. Moses found the Promised Land.'

The woman calls back. 'You think we will find a Promised Land? You are crazy. You are mixed up. Moses was not in the Book of Revelation, that Book is at the end of all things.'

The crowd behind her begins to murmur. The end of all things? Is that not where we are? Another man steps forward from behind her and pushes the first.

'You dig. If God looks after you, then you dig. Pray while you dig.'

More men join in pressing and pushing.

Kukua holds me around the waist. I can hear her whispering. 'Manu, Manu. Mama will stop them, Manu. Mama will stop them, won't she?'

I don't know what to say. I think that Kukua has forgotten that Mama died.

Or does she think that Mama's spirit is watching over us? Like Anansi in her favourite cartoon.

I want the man to dig, but I do not want to push and chant with the others. I hold tightly to Kukua's hand and we watch silently.

It feels like days since I have slept: my body doesn't know how to sleep any more. In my head Papa's stories and Gramma's stories get mixed together. I sit and lie and walk in a trance-state.

When I was very small Papa and Mr Kwame were galamseys. They hunted for mine workings that the company had decided did not contain enough gold. Papa did the hard digging and Mr Kwame used mercury to process the ore. They were proud that they found gold where the company could not. I remember Mr Kwame showing me the mercury: a silver river that flowed and swirled in his pot. I thought that one day I would join Papa and Mr Kwame but Papa read and read and he knew that the mercury was killing Mr Kwame. He wanted to join the company but how would they have him, he said? The company said the galamseys were thieves. Anyway, said Papa, they preferred to hire workers from the South, workers who learned English at the schools not on the radio.

When I was seven, the water became bad, and Papa told us, me and Mama (this was before Kukua was born), that the cyanide from the company plant had leaked. Fish floated in the water and many of us were ill. Papa told us how the company used cyanide to wash the gold out of the rocks. Fixed deep in the rock, he said, were good things, gold and silver, and bad, poisonous things, heavy metals. When the plant leaked, cyanide and heavy metals flowed in a sludge into the rivers and oozed deep into the land so that for many miles around the water played with false colours and killed anything that drank or swam. Papa helped the company clean the waters. Mama was very proud of him, and the company were proud, too, and hired him for an important job in Sekondi-Takoradi.

When the fish began to float again, a month ago, I read the books that Papa had left in Bibiani so that I could understand, and I waited for Papa and the company to come and save us again.

I remember now Gramma's old stories about the times before doctors. She would tell us about a botono who lived in her village. No-one liked to spend time with the botono. He lived apart and never worked and yet, she said, he never wanted. For the sake of an invitation into your house and a meal shared together this botono would curse your enemies. Gramma's brother wanted to marry a Dagomba girl (Gramma never said what the girl wanted). Gramma's family were Konkomba and he knew that the girl's family would never say yes, so one day Gramma's brother ran away with the girl. The girl's family asked the botono to lay a curse on him and he lay in a trance until Gramma's Mamma and Papa took him to the vodun priest. The priest called on Legba and Eshu, Sakpata and Jesus to heal Gramma's brother and on the third day he jumped up and was well and never chased the Dagomba girl again. But the girl and her family declined. The whole village knew that they had eaten with the botono, and eventually her papa grew sick and they moved south away from their tribal lands. In Gramma's stories this was always a dreadful end. But Gramma moved south too when she married, to Wasa region where, she said, she felt like a ghost. Kukua and I used to listen to these stories of Gramma. Surely, we would say, such things could never happen now.

The man scrabbles in the dirt, just scraping the surface, until someone kicks him in the ribs. 'Dig, man. Dig properly.'

We stand around, embarrassed, intent, eager. He knows there is no avoiding the digging and he begins to thrust his fingernails into the cracks and pull out great gouts of earth. He flings the waste towards the crowd and we push back, afraid even to touch the cursed soil. Even from where I stand it is clear that he has reached mud. I visualise the water seeping into the bottom of his hole. Kukua is clinging to me but I see that her eyes are fixed upon the man.

He glances at the crowd and then dips in his hand and presses it to his mouth. I can't tell for sure but the water looks clear. People shuffle forwards but I hold Kukua back.

'If the water is clean there will be enough for everyone, sister.'

She holds me tighter but her head gives a little bow of acknowledgement and I am pleased to think that she has heard me. He is drinking greedily when they reach him and push him aside. A man kneels by him and then leaps up, his hands raised in a parody of horror.

'Death water!' He turns and crawls away, pulling himself along on the legs of those who crowd around.

The man who dug has fought his way back to the hole and started to drink again. Kukua pulls on my shirt and whispers very quietly to me.

'Manu, why does he drink the bad water?'

I shake my head. 'Perhaps he thinks he will die anyway, Kukua.' She looks puzzled and I don't know whether she hasn't understood, or hasn't heard properly. Or cannot understand yet what a man maddened with thirst will do.

Already people are walking on, drifting by the man who continues kneeling over his hole, cupping his hands, filling them with water. The water swirls with blue and green and orange. He drinks deeply and splashes his face.

Scary Mary / *Hannah Styles*

If she was lucky, she found a steaming manhole cover and a cardboard mattress. If she was extra lucky, she found a St. John's Ambulance, with a sleeping bag and Cup-a-Soup.

She met David under a bridge and sucked him off. She got to cuddle up under his duvet. It was coverless, a tapestry of fag burns and mud print bodies.

They slept under the bridge for a couple of weeks, like the ugly troll. The billy goat gruffs chucked fag ends over the bridge. David collected them in a sardine tin. He said, 'Like a browsing beast, he starves if he is long away from the pavement-pasture.' He said George Orwell used to collect fag-ends with the tramps in London and Paris. George Orwell was shot in the neck, so David shot himself in the neck when he was nineteen. The hole stared at Mary and she stared at the hole. Everyone said it was infected so David stayed clear of the St. John's Ambulance. He said he would get taken to hospital and the staff would steal his possessions. David didn't have many possessions, but he always had baccy in his sardine tin and his duvet was warm.

They slept under the bridge for a couple of months. There was a lot of rain and more people started coming to the bridge. Some had Tesco trolleys and St. John's sleeping bags. Mary would cuddle up with David under their duvet and watch the other tramps having sex: moving sleeping bags, dipping heads, groans in the night.

David said they should try to get an income. George Orwell worked as a dishwasher in Hotel X. David said the Big Issue wouldn't take him back because he was on drugs. Mary shared a fag with the Romanian lady outside Superdrug, who told her to go to the Big Issue office. The lady was sweet to Mary, even though she smelt bad. She gave her some free magazines to start off with. 'You can buy the magazine at £1.25 and sell it to your customers for £2.50. You can spend the difference on whatever you like.'

Mary hung round the station all day and some of the evening for a week. She shared some money with David. They bought some heroin and some bread and they ate it without butter, under the station bridge. A drunk man wanted heroin and said he'd set the duvet on fire while they slept. Scary Mary and Duvet Dave.

One day a man with shiny leather shoes came under the bridge. He slept rough for a couple of nights and told everyone about a cult where people take clothes from shops, masturbate on them and put them back. The man got drunk with David. They kept saying 'fuck the establishment!' and 'fuck the corporations!'

The man said as long as he has his shiny shoes, they let him into all the fitting rooms. 'Imagine them, picking up a shirt, a web of jizz under the armpit. They pay a grand for that shirt and they wear my jizz out to wine bars or corporate dinners or meetings with the Bank of England. They find stains and ring up Phillip Green and tell him to go fuck himself.'

David took his duvet and said he was going with the man. George Orwell said 'human beings behave as human beings and not as cogs in the capitalist machine.'

So Mary spent all the Big Issue money on herself. She bought fake nails so her hands looked clean. She bought her own sleeping bag.

Mary heard that a homeless man was wrapped in his quilt and thrown into Tonbridge River. Everyone said it was Duvet Dave.

So Mary goes into clothes shops. As long as she has her fake nails, they let her into all the fitting rooms. As she rubs silk garments between her legs, she thinks that somewhere, David is doing similar.

Strangers at Home / *Matthew Paul*

In 1990 I stood naked in front of the full-length mirror in my parents' room and tried to see beyond the physical representation of myself. I remember it was a World Cup year because my father put his foot through the television screen when the Cameroon defender Emmanuel Kunde equalised against England.

I returned to the same mirror over and over, staring through it until I was just the imagination of myself escaping the present and no longer a boy in a bedroom shielding his ears. At times I was an imposter, running, jumping, and swimming with a body meant for someone else.

Now, on the day before my mother's funeral, I try the trick again. I stare at my reflection in the chrome fuel cap of my rental car, but it doesn't have the same effect.

Mum's funeral is scheduled for 11am at the Oakwood Crematorium & Cemetery – an inexpensive, north-facing burial plot on uneven ground. Her doctor at the nursing home assured me she left this plane at peace, and I try hard to believe her.

One of Mum's few pleasures was watching game shows and programmes set in airports. She loved to bask in other people's fleeting happiness, as if she could photosynthesise it. 'Who Wants to be a Millionaire' was her favourite; she had a system, she told me. She'd figured out the formula. But whenever contestants used their 'phone a friend' contingency she always fell silent. I would watch her from the floor and ask my general knowledge computer game why she looked sad. 'Error,' it always answered. 'If you're real, please say something,' I would ask.

You can never go home, the saying goes, and after university I took off. I will admit to doing that. It was an act that preceded thought. The problem with escaping is that you tend to forget what you're running from.

As I pull over outside what was once my local corner shop, a hooded teen scrambles for the adjacent refuse alley. The plywood board over the front window reads 'Reality Bites!' in dripping white spray-paint. He's got it all wrong. It's the dreams that'll get you, kid.

From the outside it seems our house hasn't changed much beyond the patches of Fat Hen weeds that have sprouted through the gravel drive. Beside the front porch sits a terracotta plant pot, underneath which I find the spare key, cold and blackened with grime.

Inside, I slip down the narrow corridor to the kitchen doorway where I would always be drawn by the fruits and spices of Mum's experimental cooking. Marzipan doughnuts, marmite curry, mango and asparagus pie. Comfort foods, the type of food that shuts down the cerebrum, bar the famished synapses of the pleasure centre. She had rules for eating, guidelines for maximum fulfilment. It's crucial that you're seated to fully appreciate your food; you mustn't have recently eaten garlic;

a minimum of fifteen chews per mouthful. Small lingering bites; time taken is time saved.

The grey suit I packed isn't the one she would have wanted me to wear. Mum liked the black pinstripe.

'I love this on you,' she said, 'how could anyone not hire you?'

It was the end of summer. I had a token interview for a local paper route and Mum bought me the suit with Tesco Clubcard points she was saving for Christmas. I suppose she wanted to imbue me with a sense of occasion. She said, 'Show 'em what you got,' made fists with my hands, and kissed them both.

After the interview, which consisted of a nod and a handshake, I went home in a hurry. In the kitchen, Mum was trimming my father's buzz cut with an electric razor. I flung my arms around her pregnant belly and told her I needed a new chain for my rusty BMX because I started work after school on Monday.

'You're not doing it,' my father said.

'Dad, I get seven pounds. I'll be rich.'

'You're not do-ing it,' he repeated.

'Your father thinks you're a little young,' Mum said.

'I'm thirteen,' I said. 'I know how to get the bus to town and everything.'

'Ryan, that's the end of it,' he said, almost in one elongated word. I was close enough to smell the lubricant on the steel shaver head; its hornets' nest whine filled the room, and when I said Mum, Mum, Mum, the words were lost in the din.

The sound collapsed as the razor head cracked from being launched against the wall, and he was standing squared up to me with his chest puffed out. He was a man who inhabited a lot of space. He said, 'When I say that's the end of it, what does that mean?' I bit through the skin on my lip and ran to my room.

'Maybe next year, love,' I heard Mum call upstairs.

Years later she let slip that he owed the shop owner hundreds of pounds on lost bets.

I should be wearing the pinstripe suit.

Greeting me in place of Mum's cooking is a curious fog of cinnamon, cigarettes and body odour. The stink comes from my father slouching over the table; he is whey-skinned, with patches under his eyes like he'd caught a one-two punch. A thick crust of Richmond cigarette ash eclipses the china saucer in front of him. Weathered hinges from the neighbour's swing squeal and scrape as a child launches from the ground.

'You look like I could use a drink,' he says and retrieves from under his chair a tumbler and near-empty bottle of supermarket whiskey. The one element of control Mum had was to disallow him to booze it up in the house. He must have habitually hidden his stash when he heard the key in the door.

'How are you, Dad?' I ask.

'My wife died.'

He downs the contents of the glass and judders into a hacking cough. I think about getting him some water. I think about rubbing his back. I think lots of things. He asks me how the hell I think he feels, and I sit across from him and say I'm sorry.

I notice his hands. Scraped, jagged, mottled, permanently engraved with working-class graft. He glances around, trying to remember his hiding places for alcohol. I stop scraping my split thumbnail across my thigh before it draws attention. He's careful not to clink his glass against the table as he sets it down.

We watch a spider scuttle across the table and come to a stop at the glass. My father takes a lingering draw from a Richmond cigarette, blows the smoke inside and imprisons the spider underneath it.

'Your brother asleep?' he says.

'I wanted to see you first.'

'You shouldn't keep him up.'

The swing outside picks up a steady rhythm.

'If he's tired tomorrow he won't stay still. Don't want him freaking out in front of everyone.' He stubs out his cigarette and pats his shirt pocket in search of another.

'I won't keep him awake.'

'Goddamnit, where are they?'

'He doesn't freak out, Dad.'

'I just had 'em,' he says.

'Dad, Max doesn't freak out.'

His tendency to marginalise Max's illness seems to grant a sort of buffer between coping and despair, a margin of error. The swing's frame yawns as the neighbour's child reaches a fleeting apex. It's all downhill from there, kid.

'Right here they were,' he says, 'bastards always disappear when I need 'em most.'

'Mummy,' my brother Max wails from the bedroom. Mum had chicken pox during the pregnancy and he was born with autism. His mental acuity will never reach adolescence. In that regard it's tough to discern how he's different from the rest of us.

'Shall I go?' I ask my father for both our sakes. He looks about ready to tip his bartender. I see my opening for a jab.

'Whatever you're looking for,' I say, nudging the bottle, 'you won't find it at the bottom.'

'Not before I get there, anyway.'

'Mummy,' Max wails again.

'Hey, Ryan?' He finds the cigarettes under his chair and smacks the pack against his palm. 'She left three messages for you last week.' I free the spider from custody and it weaves an uncertain path back the way it came. I follow its example.

Ivory paint flakes off the banister into my hand as I skirt the sunken floorboards on the stairs so as not to wake Max. The family photographs hung parallel are a forged pageantry.

Max had been waiting. He jumps out from the bottom bunk and hugs me with unexpected force. He asks for a story and I read a pop-up book about fire engines twice through.

'Do you know what a secret is?' I ask him.

'I got lots of those that all my friends tell me I'm really good at.'

'Has Dad been drinking while I was away?'

'You were away a long time like those people in space.'

'That's right, I was.'

'Mum says you went away because you were sad,' he says. There's a loose wire in Max's conversation. He forgets what he's said if you stay silent for a few seconds. I'm not proud of this tactic, but what is it they say about needs must? He asks me for apple juice.

'Maybe in the morning, Maximillion,'

'OK, Ryan-a-million. I'll have some tomorrow, Ryan-a-million.'

'Time for sleep. Big day tomorrow.'

'Big, massive, *huge* day. The biggest day in the world. I'm really good at sleeping.'

'I know you are, buddy. Lights out.'

Max *is* good at sleeping. I abandon the top bunk to get some air. Outside, a group of women garble the lyrics to a song played on a mobile phone; their crowing and clattering heels echo into the distance. A man in a torn shirt strides past wringing a hammer between his hands. Parked nearby are three police vans and an ambulance with a paramedic asleep at the wheel. I walk further.

The shaft of light from a lamppost highlights a condemned building where shadows of moths decorate the walls. I walk past it in the road because I can. Leering billboards make promises of whiter smiles and cars on affordable finance plans. A slight figure occupies the window on the tenth floor of a block of flats, and I wave to it. It was an action that preceded thought. The shape hauls the window down and retreats into the room which goes dark. A torch is aimed at my face from the passenger seat of a police car as it coasts by. I turn back.

On the corner of my street, two policemen bundle the hammer guy into the back of their car; one of the women bends over her stilettos, heaving at the drain.

Mum insisted that our kitchen door should never be closed, saying something about it being the focal point of a home. But the door is shut, like there's been a correction now that she's gone, and behind it is a muffled sound of despair. My conscience nudges me inside.

My father sits facing the door, a lethargic silhouette against the glow from the neighbour's security lamp. He's writhing or undulating or crying. I flick the light.

His trousers are bunched at his ankles. A blonde with an Ouroboros tattoo on her nape sits astride him, her tie-dye dress hitched up waist height. From the drool daubed across his neck he looks to have passed out at some point. I'm already applying hindsight to these next moments and congratulating myself on doing the right thing.

But in my experience, presence of mind is a hard thing to come by.

You fall into a sort of altered state when you see things you can't explain. Like the mirror, the image in front of me reflected a reality I couldn't frame. I was half-awake, or trying to articulate a dream only half remembered. I lay on the linoleum as it was the only thing left to do. She left. The hooker left. There must have been advanced payment but perhaps she wasn't what I presumed her to be.

The grief came, and it too escaped before I could stop it.

I start to pull his trousers up. Max can't see him slumped in a chair, flaccid from head-to-toe. This is the person upon whom Max has to depend. Coins from his pockets fall. I wonder if hookers give change.

'Where did she go?' he says, unmoved.

'She's gone.'

'Why?'

'Took her money and left,' I say. 'Want her back so she can get you off?'

'You made her go, Ryan.'

'She had no business being here.'

'She loved you more than I could and you made her quit waiting,' he says. 'Where the hell have you been?'

We are both on the ground now — him leaning against the counter, me on my knees in the middle of the room. I'd been waiting for this confrontation, but I'm still unprepared.

'My father was a real asshole, Ryan, a fire and brimstone Catholic.'

He goes on. He was beaten as a child as he battled against a strict religious doctrine and always lost. 'Like sticking two fingers up to God and getting slapped by the devil,' he says.

I can see he's fading. He says, 'I did what I thought best for you and Max but failed,' and crumples into pieces onto the floor. I didn't so much as throw a jab.

Back in my bunk, I dream about the funeral. A four-gun salute takes aim and a chef wearing Michelin star epaulettes hands me a folded tablecloth. One of the gunmen removes a hip-flask from his breast pocket, downs the contents, breaks rank and points the barrel towards me. The casket stirs. The gunmen make up the brass section of a philharmonic playing Dance Macabre and my father moves his aim to the coffin that shakes and threatens to throw open the lid and I'm here but I'm distant now; I'm watching from a blast shelter through safety goggles, dreading the mushroom cloud, and my finger is on the button that reads push me and I stay silent for a few seconds until the explosion forgets its purpose but it doesn't; my father stands next to me saying 'out of sight' in a whisper that screams and I see her: Mum stands in the open and I think of monochrome photos of the fallout where the trees are analogous to the dirt and I say stop but a red button must be pushed and he counts 10, 9, 8, 7, there's time, I can save her but a red button must be pushed — 6, 5, 4 — she struggles with the weight of a silver serving tray carrying my father who eats warm banana mince pies and I know I should be out there with her, bearing the load, but I can't cope, I'm still the child and I can't deal with it so I leave the blast shelter and run so hard but I go nowhere, I'm sinking through the earth then crash through wood into a coffin, lined with deluxe ivory padding, that shakes — 3, 2 — and next to me is Mum smiling, vomiting up dozens of white pills — 1, 0 — everything turns black and I can hear the war planes outside but it's all moving too fast to fix a point and I can't bear to be involved; I'm temporarily Switzerland and this is what it's like to be alone.

Max has to slouch to fasten my tie in the morning, doing so with intense concentration. I bought a clip-on but dismissed it. Then I changed my mind and thought of how absurd it was that I was making the funeral about my choice of tie. If Mum were there she'd be the first to insist on not faking it with a clip-on. She will be there, of course — the sole attendee not on the guest list.

'Are we going to a party?' Max asks. I don't know what to say that would make sense to both of us, and I need to check on Dad.

Instead of lying prone on the floor as I expect, he's showered and dressed and standing in front of the bedroom mirror.

'You used to do this,' he says, 'watch yourself for hours.'

'There's coffee made.'

'You were trying to bulk up, weren't you? Take me down.'

'That's not what I was doing, Dad.'

'Help Max,' he says. 'Let's get this over with.'

Let's get this over with, I think, and struggle to disagree.

Max has dressed himself. I didn't know he could do that. He asks if it's his birthday but I don't know that, either. I play the odds and tell him it's not. We go downstairs for coffee and apple juice.

'Are you still sad?' he says.

'I am today.'

'I lost my army man outside and cried and there was a rock that was black and shiny and then I was okay.'

'You don't miss your army man?' I ask.

'I didn't play with it much, anyway.'

The car pulls up outside and I leave the spare key under the pot. In the doorway of a house across the street stands a woman wearing a white dressing-gown. A man comes from behind, drinking from a black mug and scanning a magazine as he joins her there. She cries. I think about how she's trying to hijack my Mum's death, muscling in on our loss so she can vent her own troubles. I think a lot of things.

I think a stranger has no right to grieve, no cause to say goodbye.

The Tumour / *Hannah Meads*

There's, like, this *bulge*, in our bathroom wall. Right opposite the toilet so you pretty much have to look at it whenever you go. I'm not talking the size of a paint bubble, or a golf ball, or anything minor like that; I'm talking metre-high, ten inches out. I can't bring myself to touch it. I stand and I stare at it, waiting for it to do something. I ask myself what I have to gain by touching it – the answer is nothing. Trouble is, I get the same answer when I question what I have to lose.

I feel like there's something in there: a child; an old pet; a body, its hands stretching out of the wall like Han Solo frozen in carbonite. Then I scold myself for being so melodramatic. I wonder sometimes if it's maybe possible for wallpaper to buckle, as it were, and get painted over so that it's permanently sticking out. I wonder sometimes whether, on the opposite side, next door has a hole in their wall, and whether they store stuff in it. It'd make a nice alcove for a candle holder or something like that.

Of course, the first thing that comes to mind at five a.m. is, 'Oh God oh fuck it's a body oh GOD even worse it's alive and it's going to crawl out and kill me while my trousers are round my ankles.' And all the ways I'd want to die are far more glamorous than that.

I'd move if I didn't love the rest of the house so much. It was Gran's 'spare house,' and when she died she left it to me and my sister, Jules. When we moved in, the wallpaper in the downstairs bedroom contained six shades of brown. That was the first thing of many that we changed, and now, if it weren't for that bulge, everything would be perfect.

Last thing Gran ever said to me was, 'Mel, don't you ever get this old. Don't you ever be eighty-three. There's no joy in it.' If she'd died in this house, I'd think the bulge was her. It's cruel, but sometimes I wish Jules, not me, had found Gran. I just feel like she could've dealt with it better, like she'd've known what to do. Me, I just walked away and closed the door and sat on the floor and cried. I sat in that house for two hours until Jules came in from work and saw my face. She asked if something had happened to Gran. I nodded and my face acted like it was crying, twitching and making my mouth dry, but I was out of tears.

At the autopsy, they found a cancerous tumour. Said with that plus her heart condition, she hadn't stood a chance. We found her heart pills in her room later when we were sorting through her things. She hadn't taken them for a week before she died.

I spend a lot of time alone. While Jules is out at work, I sit at home, watch TV, read the internet, often at the same time. Having the TV on gives me someone to converse with. There was a documentary on about the human body narrated by some smug looking guy in a cardigan. They were filming a guy getting a double hand transplant, apparently the first ever. I reckon it'd feel like wearing really heavy gloves, or like when, at the beach, your big sister buries your hands in the sand. Could he feel with them? Apparently, yes. Oh, God, they were taking out the veins, piling them up next to the newly-severed hand. They looked like bits of mincemeat. The hands looked plastic, bad props in a zombie flick. When they attached them to him he looked like Frankenstein's monster, red scars criss-crossed over his new hands. There was a weird bulge sticking out of his wrist. This man had corpse hands sewn onto his body, and he had given them life again. The flesh tones didn't quite match up and they were greenish and sickly in comparison.

Does Jules know about the bulge? She must have noticed, surely. You can't just miss a bloody great lump in the middle of the bathroom. She knows, and she doesn't want to scare me. We'll talk about it tomorrow, over breakfast. I take the torch next to my bed and attempt to read, but the words blur into one. That usually means it's a dream, doesn't it? It's a way to test if you're dreaming: you try to read and if the words change, it's a dream. The words stay in place now.

The torchlight makes my fingers glow bright red when it passes through them. I check to see if my bones show up. No luck. Maybe I don't have bones, and *my* hand is just a cheap stage prop. No, I have bones. I've seen one of them, when it popped out of my arm when I was eleven and I jumped over a fence badly on my paper round. I expected it to be pure white, but it was covered in blood, which was also a darker red than I'd anticipated. When I think of the thing bursting out of the wall, it's that shade of red, and its bones pierce the skin the same way. Once I start to think about it, I can't stop. I imagine it reaching out and clawing at me, trying to drag me in there, trying to *turn me into it*. I imagine trying to fight back with whatever's nearby, but there's nothing nearby (I make a mental note, here, to keep something strong and swingable in the bathroom – a baseball bat, say). I imagine that I grab the bat and I hit it, over and over, and it screeches with a sound that *is* pain, and I go for the eyes but *it has no eyes*.

When I wake up, it's dark. Fuck winter. I walk to the bathroom, wishing I'd worn socks to bed as the cold creeps up my legs. I switch on the light and it's there, cutting into the world, angular and wrong, in shadow and bright. I pretend it isn't there. I walk to the sink to wash my hands. It's a few inches from my head now. There's something weird(er) about it today – like it's grown. There's a gap in the plaster, and I can't help it: I have to see. I leave the tap on, like that'll trick it, or just so that I'm not in silence any more. I lean in, I rest my hand on the uncorrupted wall beside it, and I can hear the violins getting faster and faster as you all cry, 'No! Don't!' but still I go to press my eye against the gap, expecting there to be light inside, knowing that whatever's in there is something I don't want to see. But I *do*. The wall is warm. I look inside.

Scores for Porn / *Rosie Riches*

'Isaac? It's John.'

'John....' Isaac and John were the only people queued at the till in WH Smith and there was no one serving. The shop had opened for the day a few minutes before. The smell of pencil shavings and new books was thick like the air in a spice market.

'Yes, we met at the chicken talk last week.'

'Oh, John. Sorry. Yeah. How's you?'

'Not bad.'

'Good, good. Sorry about this. The lady just went upstairs to fetch an order for me. I'm making you late.'

'No, it's no problem. I don't start work for another hour and a half. That's plenty of time. I only work in the bank around—'

'Ah, okay. It's a long time to wait to buy a paper though, isn't it?'

'No problem.' John picked at his fingernails having noticed a distance in his queue companion's eyes. On their first meeting John had guessed Isaac was a few years younger than himself, maybe late thirties, but at this time of the morning it was hard to tell. Isaac's fair hair was fluffy and he looked as though he could sleep where he stood. John cleared his throat as a silence began to open up between them.

'You know...I'm really having difficulties with my hens.'

'Oh really?' Isaac yawned and smiled, blinking.

'Yeah, they really don't seem happy. I mean, I've tried so hard, gave them all the space I could but—'

'Well, there's your problem.'

'What?'

'The space. You said they were ex-battery, right?'

'Yeah.'

'Well, they're probably a bit agoraphobic, you know.'

'OK. What would you suggest?'

'Hmm, I'll have to think about that. My girls were never shut up like that. I know hens though. You think it'll all be simple but sometimes it's like looking after a coop of mental patients.'

'Yeah, but it keeps me occupied at least. After the wife left I—'

'Why don't you come over to my place this weekend if you're free? I can show you my set up and give you some advice.'

'How about tomorrow?'

'I work Saturday mornings but I'll be home by one.'

'That sounds good.'

'Here.' Isaac picked up a biro from a tub on the desk and took John's newspaper to scribble down a phone number and address.

'So, where do you work?'

'You know the Subway Sandwich just round the corner from here?'

'Yeah?'

'In there.'

'Manager?'

'Hell no. One of the guys that makes sandwiches. The company likes to call us sandwich artists.'

'Really?'

'Yeah.' Isaac laughed. 'It gives me enough to live though. You know? Ah, here she is.'

A young woman slipped in behind the desk and glittered at Isaac in such a way that John wondered if she knew him intimately.

'Sorry about the wait, sir. Here's your magazines.' There were about thirty magazines tied in a bundle with string. John tilted his head to read the spines and realised they were all the same magazine: *Barely Legal Vol. 103.* He looked at Isaac for some explanation but received the sort of smile you would expect from a charity worker.

'I'll see you around, John. Just give me a call if you can't find it.'

'Sure. Thanks. Isaac.'

Isaac walked from the shop with his back straight, gripping his purchase by the string.

'Do you know him?' John asked as he counted coins in his palm for his newspaper and handed them over to the woman.

'No,' she said, 'is he a friend of yours?'

'No, well, I met him recently.'

When he stepped outside a freezing fog had knocked the town centre out of focus and the air was still fresh before the day's traffic had dirtied it. The street was quiet apart from a woman's heels clicking on the pavement. John went to Starbucks and sat at the window to sip black coffee and stare at the grey building where he worked as a cashier. As he waited for security to open the door his mind clicked back eighteen months to shortly after his wife, Hilary, had left him. John was waiting to cross the road to get from the car park to the centre of town. His mind was drawn to an argument that had happened over a month before. They had been in the kitchen quarrelling about who should get custody over the dog. John pointed out that Hilary had a new pet, her boyfriend Douglas, so John should at least get the dog. As Hilary pulled the toaster from the plug socket and prepared to launch it, John stepped out in front of the 105 to Painswick.

The surgeons told John he was lucky the bus had only glanced him or he might have died. John had several abrasions and a compound fracture to his left tibia. Through the wool of opiates, John could not understand what compound fractions had to do with anything until the consultant pulled back the sheets and John saw bone jutting through a ragged gash. He could see then that even the fractured fractions of his bone had been splintered into fractions. John blacked out and when he woke up his tibia was back inside him. Metal halos surrounded his leg and were held in place by rods that sprouted from his flesh.

The first week had been a struggle but John soon came to enjoy the attention he received and the painkillers that wrapped him in clouds. He was sad when he was discharged but once back at home he found his time was his own. John felt eight years old again. Built up repetitive misery, to which he had become accustomed, sloughed away. He ate what he wanted, slept when he wanted, and bought a PlayStation, losing whole days playing Tekken and Metal Gear Solid. Soon John's bone began to heal. After several hospital appointments showing his strong recovery, the bank insisted he should return to his job as soon as possible. The halos came off, the rods were uprooted, and John was forced back into a routine.

John felt the welts beneath his grey suit trousers. The surgeons had done the best they could to make his leg normal but John missed his rods and halos. Every weekday he crossed the road from the car park to the town centre and ached for the 105 to crush his bones to compound fractions again. This was why he had decided to branch out a bit, get a hobby of some kind. A rotund work colleague named Nikki talked him into keeping chickens. He was beginning to think this had been a bad idea.

John stood in watery December sun on the doorstep of the small cottage that was situated about two miles out of town. He had driven there in his Mercedes, its bulk filling the country lanes. Now it stood black and hard against the muted greens and browns of its surroundings. He pressed the doorbell and hoped that the occupant was not in. The door opened and Isaac grinned out at him.

'John, you made it. Come in.'

Isaac shuffled up the hallway in a pair of red socks and John stood fumbling with the laces on his shiny shoes.

'Oh, don't worry about taking those off,' Isaac called to him.

'It's okay, they're nearly off.' John levered the shoes from his feet and left them where they fell.

'Do you live here on your own?' John said as he passed through the clutter-free hallway and into a clean kitchen.

'Yeah.'

'You own?'

'What?'

'The cottage. Is it yours?'

'No, no way.' He laughed. 'Can you imagine how many shifts I would have to do at Subway to afford a house? No, it's better this way. The landlord sorts out repairs, all that sort of crap, and I just keep it warm for him. Coffee? Tea?'

'Coffee, thanks.'

'Take a seat,' Isaac said as he put the kettle on and got a packet of fresh coffee from the fridge. John sat at the large oak table. The table appeared to be the only thing in disarray. There was a big square board on it and hundreds of bits of glossy paper arranged in small heaps. There was also a modelling scalpel, glue, and some sort of arts and craft varnish.

'What are you making here?' John said over the boiling kettle as he tried to make out the images on the bits of paper.

'3D decoupage.'

'Decoupage?'

'Yeah, 3D. You take loads of duplicates of the same picture and build up certain parts of it, gluing on pieces over the top of other pieces to give a sort of 3D effect.'

'Oh, yeah, yeah, I know what you mean. My mum used to do a bit of it. She used to do pictures of owls and things and enter them into art and craft competitions.'

'That's it.' Isaac stirred the coffee in a small cafetiere.

'So what's the picture of?' John stood up and tilted his head to centralise the image that was beginning to take shape on a sheet of card. 'Oh. I see.'

Isaac chuckled as he brought over the cafetiére, two mugs, and cream and sugar on a tray. 'Really is quite an unflattering pose, isn't it?'

The two men sat down. Isaac began shovelling teaspoons of sugar into his coffee – John counted at least five – and then poured in cream until the drink looked more like a milky cup of tea. John's eyes wandered back over to the decoupage.

'What got you into decoupage, then?' John said and then wondered whether he should have glossed over this apparently obsessive hobby.

'Seemed like something interesting to do.'

'Why that particular subject? Are you a porn fan?'

'When I was a teenager, sure, definitely I was. Which boy isn't?'

'Well—'

'But now, it seems to me as if it's too much, you know? It gives too much away.'

'Yeah.'

'I suppose that doesn't answer your question, does it?'

'Not entirely.'

'I kind of wanted to see how it would affect me. I didn't know if it was possible to put so much concentration in the minute detail of a cunt.'

'I suppose that could be—'

'It was odd though. I stopped seeing the sleaziness. It became something else.' The two men sipped their coffees.

'Like a flower?' John ventured, beginning to think that the conversation might reveal a serious instability in Isaac's personality.

'No! Come on, a flower? When I took it to pieces it became, well, pieces. It was the same as any other picture would be if you cut out all the different elements. It might as well have been a Beatrix Potter illustration.'

'I suppose when you finished it will be a cu…vagina again though.'

'To the onlooker, maybe. I don't think I'll ever see it that way again though. Maybe some other people looking at it might appreciate that too. The building blocks. Just a picture made up of building blocks that happen to resemble something we consider rude.'

'I'm not sure the WI will see it that way.'

'You're probably right there,' Isaac said, laughing.

'Will you enter it in a competition?'

'Yeah, why not? I don't expect to win. In fact, I expect I might get thrown out, but it's all good fun.'

After they finished their coffees in a pillow of silence, Isaac clapped his hands together and John flinched.

'Right, shall we go and look at these birds then?'

'Birds? Oh right. Yes.' John had forgotten about the chickens.

There was a back door in the kitchen. It was covered in peeling white paint and had a window in it that was frosted with a leaf design. The key was already resting in the lock and Isaac unlocked and opened the door allowing the cold sunshine to leak across the terracotta-tiled floor. John could hear the clucking of the hens coming from the bottom of the lawn.

'It's a nice day, isn't it?' Isaac said, stepping out onto a small patio in his socks. John nodded and craned to look behind him, realising that he had left his shoes by the front door. He decided that going to put his shoes on might cause a rift between him and his host, so he followed Isaac. The paving slabs sucked the heat from his feet and the cold flickered up through his body and into his molars. He hunched his shoulders and thrust his hands into his pockets and crossed over to the damp lawn. His socks were saturated by the time the two men reached the coop next to a potting shed.

'So here are my girls,' Isaac said, his cheeks pink with freshness. 'I'll let them out so you can have a look at them. I usually let them out in the day but they always have to go back in before it gets dark. The foxes aren't fussy like us. They'll eat them no worries.' He flicked three latches on the edge of the large coop and the hens bobbed out, spreading across the grass. Each one of them seemed to have a serious defect: clubbed feet, strange angled necks, ugly growths, and missing eyes. On top of these serious flaws, most of them had bald patches where their pink skin shone out and John was reminded of the rows of chickens on supermarket shelves.

'I know what you're thinking,' Isaac said as he grinned at John.

'You do?'

'Yes, you're thinking *why would anyone want to look after such revolting creatures?* Am I right?'

'Well, I suppose you get the eggs. It doesn't matter what they look like.'

'Nope. Do these birds look like they could lay eggs? None of them lay.'

'They don't?'

'Nope.'

'In that case, no. I have no idea why you would want to keep these creatures.'

'I don't really know either. I like them though.'

'They're ex-battery?'

'No. Well, sort of. They came from a battery farm, but these hens were thrown out before they were even put in cages.'

'Oh, rejects.'

'Yup. So they didn't have the problems that yours are having right now.'

'What do you think I should do with them?'

'I suggest you take it slowly. Reduce the size of the coop by half. When they seem to be happy with that then you can expand it, little by little.'

'That sounds like a good plan.'

'Having never kept hens that have been cooped up for so long like yours, I'm not sure how they will cope. I don't know if they will ever be happy being out of their cage altogether. Hopefully over time they will be running about your lawn the same way mine do.'

'I did try to let them out. They stood there blinking and shaking.'

'I don't envy those animals. It's not only their freedom that has been taken, but, I suppose, some fundamental right to be, well, a chicken.'

'That isn't a good existence.'

'No. You're doing a good thing for them. Unlike yours, my hens are lucky bastards.'

John watched as the chickens hobbled and dragged their bodies across the lawn. They pecked at the ground a little and stared at one another with bewilderment as Isaac fought with the bolt on the shed. He muttered to himself as he wiggled the bolt and clattered the metal from side to side. He finally got in and came out with a bag of feed, covered in cobwebs and dust.

'Lucky?' John said.

'Oh, it might not seem that way, granted,' said Isaac. 'I mean, look at the fucking state of them.'

'They are...something else, that's for sure.'

'I'd be happy as one of these girlies though. They've got it good. No one ever expected a damn thing from them. They were free from the moment they hatched.'

'I suppose there is that.'

'And put it this way, if they were all plump, healthy, and feathery, I would be licking my lips, like Mr Fox, and sharpening my axe.'

'That is true.' John looked askance at Isaac plunging his hand into the sack of feed and scattering it around the lawn as he made bubbly *chuck-chuck* noises. Isaac's face was relaxed, the corners of his mouth upturned.

'You really have got it good though, haven't you?' said John.

Isaac stopped throwing seed and met John's eye. His face split into a wide grin. 'Don't I know it,' he said and started to laugh.

At eleven in the morning, John sat on the bench in front of the bank and started to look through his newspaper for the job section. It was nearly Christmas and the town's lights had been strung above the streets, glittering and happy. He turned the pages and saw a face he recognised. It was a photo of Isaac next to his decoupage in the Tate Modern. The vagina had been pixelated out. Isaac was staring straight into the camera and smiling, the same relaxed smile that John had seen in the garden that Saturday afternoon. A big dealer in the art world stood next to him in a smart suit and lavish jewellery, not looking at the camera but studying Isaac.

John felt the knotty muscles in his shoulders begin to untie. The bank had taken his resignation well, to the point that John suspected they did not really need him there at all. He had no plan of what to do next. Maybe he would get a job as a park keeper, or failing that he could be a coffee artist in Starbucks. He ripped out the page with Isaac's photo and the accompanying article, which described Isaac's rise to infamy following his forceful removal from a WI arts and craft fair. John folded the page and tucked it in his suit pocket. As he walked in the direction of the car park, he threw the rest of the newspaper in the bin. There would be plenty of time to look for a job tomorrow, he thought. Before he crossed the road, John waited while the 105 to Painswick passed him by.

Collecting Flashes / *Synnøve Hjortland Carlsen*

When I was seven years old and dad came back from the toilet, I sat in our red faux-leather armchair, that would recline if you had long enough legs to reach the floor, and asked one of the questions that have always come back to me: Dad, do you stand up when you go to the toilet?

First he looked at me, then at mum who coughed into her coffee, and then he answered: No, not any more. Only boys stand up.

Then he winked at me and asked why I wondered, but I only shrugged my shoulders and smiled at him. From that time forwards, I would always think 'he is a boy then' whenever I heard someone splashing piss in the toilet from a distance.

⁎

The third week I was dropped off at Sindre's house was the first time I saw 'it.' His mum, Charlotte, was my 'nine 'til four' mum. That's how we got to know each other. We used to play in his garden. He had a trampoline with a net, so we could play football. We had been lying on the ground by his house, as close as we were allowed near the big tractor that was digging dirt away from the little hillside by their house. Sindre had said they were building a playground, but last time we had Brussels sprouts for dinner Charlotte said it was going to be a lawn, so I wasn't sure whom I believed.

I need a piss, said Sindre.

Sindre said 'piss' with a grin. As if I found him cool. I could say piss too. He got up so I followed. The pile of dirt the tractor had dug had little patches of grass growing from it. It could turn out to be a pretty nice pile in the end if they left it. Sindre walked around it so the windows couldn't see us and stuck his hand down his pants and pulled his 'it' out.

Is that what it looks like? I said. I bent down to look closer. It was short. It looked like a finger without a nail, and it had an extra set of skin on the outside that didn't seem to stretch quite far enough. It created a little circle, and the inside stuck out like it did in his navel.

Yeah, and you can do this, see? Sindre put his fingers around the tip of it and pushed the extra skin around it down as far as it would go. With the thing in his hands he waved it around in a circle. See? he said again. Just like a sausage.

The old Barbie Ken I found under Jørgen's bed didn't have that. Raw sausage.

He told me to leave so he could 'do his thing.' I stayed, but nothing interesting happened. Then, for as long as there was sunshine, we sat on the dirt pile, smelling the fish fingers that swam on the breeze from the dinner window.

⁎

Do you see these potatoes? Charlotte held up a potato with a chequered tea towel. We were sitting around the table in their kitchen. It was oval-shaped, longer and lighter in colour than the red potatoes we usually had at home — it was just about the colour of Sindre's piss when he drank a lot of water. Charlotte twisted it around in the tea towel and dried it off as she continued: These potatoes are called 'Charlotte Potatoes.' They have the same name as me, which means I have been named after them.

You don't look much the same.

It is the *meaning* of the name that is similar to me; it means feminine and little. They stay firm if you cook them, and they are very nice in salads. Your name, Synnøve, means 'gift from the sun.' Sindre's name means 'spark.'

Feminine?

Mhm, she said.

I liked that. I decided to remember that.

About this time, I met Sindre's neighbour Regine. I didn't know it then, but we would end up in the same class at school later that year. She had a snail farm by her house that we had to keep the slugs out of, and she said she'd teach me how to live, that I wasn't wild enough. I was wild by climbing high up in trees to build tree-houses, I told her. I was so wild the boys down the street wouldn't let me play football anymore. She meant illegal stuff. She was wilder than me, she said.

One day, I took her to a house where the roof was so low you could jump on to it straight from the ground. We climbed to the top where the two sides met. There we sat, straddling the rooftop, and chatted about who invented the kissing game in preschool.

There was a balcony to the right of the house, and we managed to drop down to it. The door was locked, and there were flies and longlegs in the window we looked through. There was a brown chair to the side wall and a rug on the floor, a bed with two pillows and a table with a cup. The whole room looked light-brown, the dust in the air made it hard to see the wall on the other side. We could smell mould and moth droppings through a crack in the door.

The sound must be paper wasps, said Regine.

Regine knew things like that because she liked to poke spiderwebs with a straw, so the spider in the middle would spin around and become a ball of beige, until we could no longer see the little cross it carried on its back. Regine sometimes put woodlice on her arm when we went to the shop.

We never found out which of us was the wildest. I told dad about the stuff we did. He always laughed. One time he suggested we were wildest together.

Once, when it was raining, Regine and I sat inside someone's shed. It was her idea; she said no one would come out to check in such bad weather. She had a white bag filled with salty liquorice crocodiles, and sucked on the tail of one while we watched the rain beat down straws and unlucky birds that didn't get to the right tree in time and had to fly back out. She finished her crocodile and got out a new one.

Are you going to share with me? I asked.

No.

Why not?

They're mine.

I remembered when mum talked to me and my sister about 'behaviour like that,' and her reply then had been the exact same as my reply was now; I don't like people that can't share.

Regine looked at me and then into her bag before she got a crocodile out and pulled half a tail off and handed it to me. Half a tail.

Share properly. If you don't share fairly I'm going to leave.

That was what mum had told me to say. Regine rammed her hand into her bag and produced three crocodiles. She stuck them all into my hands. I was surprised; I didn't expect her to share more than one.

Thank you.

We smiled at each other. I didn't actually like liquorice. We sat watching the rain again and chewed on our crocodiles.

∷

Five days after I crashed into Sindre's wall with my bike and broke one of his dad's new rosebushes, we were out in our raincoats. We wore our wellies, mine were decorated with flowers, and we were playing in the slushy snow that the ploughing-machine had scooped out to the sides earlier that morning.

Hey! His dad was walking towards us in big strides, past the salt-box, which was standing by the door, and through the labyrinth of puddles to where we were playing treasure hunt. OK, you three. Listen to me. First of all, stop digging holes in my gravel; second of all, the rocks by the living room window are very sharp. The ice has made them slippery. Don't go up there. OK?

I went up there. I balanced fine until I looked down on Sindre and Regine. Then I fell, and I remember the sharp stone coming straight at me. Straight into my forehead. I don't know if I lay there for long, but when I got back up and climbed down to them, they were both staring at me.

What? So it's true it's slippery. I feel fine.

Look at your raincoat.

I wiped rain out of my eyes and it turned my hand red. I looked down at my raincoat and it had thick trails of blood running down it. Regine lifted her hand and pointed at my forehead. I lifted my hand to feel it, but there was nothing there.

I think maybe you should go home.

Sindre ran ahead, screaming for Charlotte. I didn't know what was going on, but I felt fine. Regine took my hand and dragged me along. I kept wiping my eyes and my mouth tasted of rust.

What have you done? Charlotte lifted me up and carried me into the house, up the stairs and into the kitchen. I was put on a stool and she started wiping my head with the chequered potato towel. Sindre and Regine were standing in the kitchen doorway.

I want to see, I said.

Charlotte didn't take any notice of me; she just kept wiping my forehead.

I want to see, Charlotte.

Magnus, can you call Frida and tell her to come pick up Synnøve?

Charlotte. I want to see.

Finally she looked at me. She wiped my head again a few times and said: Go on then. You might as well.

I walked to the bathroom mirror with my eyes closed, following the path I had walked every day for a year. The tiles warmed me through my socks as I stopped in front of the mirror. My hands were damp when I removed them from my face. When I opened my eyes a gaping gash screamed back at me, its mouth wider than mine. I ran back to Charlotte, crying, and when mum arrived they had a massive argument about what I had been shown.

The Exorcised / *Richard Steele*

I don't know exactly how old I was when they exorcised me. For the sake of this story I will say I was thirteen – it couldn't have been long before this, or long after. Thirteen feels like a nice place to begin, and it's not like you know how old I was, so I can do pretty much whatever I like. So where do I start? How do you create a concrete autobiographical piece when your memory is so hazy? Maybe I should start with a bit of character development....

I was chubby.

When it rained, I would ride my bike[18] around the block for an hour, wondering why no one braved the rain. Why life outside ceased to exist. Why wearing plastic-toy-chest-armour under two tops (one waterproof) and two pairs of jeans and Cica trainers[19] would keep you, inevitably, dry. Why no-one loved *Lord of the Rings* as much as I did. And why I had no girlfriend.[20] I would imagine that I was on some trusted steed – Shadowfax or Black Beauty – galloping my glorious escape from the Orcs of Mordor.

Often, after such a rainy Sunday morning ride, I would go to church for some singing, sermons and prayer. It's embarrassing to admit that I was a God-loving, constantly praying, 'Jesus loves you,' priest-aspiring, kind of youth. I feel like I'm admitting to a sordid past, some time in my life when I was ruled by my stupidity and general ignorance.

I wore shell suits.

So now that you've been fed some character development, let us get back to the story before you lose interest.[21]

You probably noticed that I planted a hook in you at the start of the first paragraph, a nice juicy hook that is, I hope, yanking on your subconscious. You've fallen for the bait – you've tasted a bit of unnecessary back-story and let this rambling narration imbed itself in your mind. I will now attempt to reel you in.

I recently had a conversation with my Mum in which I asked for details as research for this story:

Me: Alright?

Mum: Yeah, [yawn] I'm a bit tired. You just caught me; I was about to go to bed.

---

18   One of those amazing bikes with a computeresque-style dashboard which had ten buttons you could press while riding. Each one would create a sound stolen from an eighties sci-fi film: a peow peow laser, a du-du-du-du-du from a machine gun, a monolithic explosion noise and various other crackling, speaker-spewed decibels that sounded so much better when I was younger.

19   Don't ask.

20   In retrospect, I know why.

21   I have all the 'so-called-writing-rules' niggling at me, telling me I've spent seven hundred and twenty nine (more by now) words introducing the story and character; 'Chekov's Razor' might end up cropping my introduction-side-burns. It's interesting to note that at this point the word count is actually four hundred and forty five. That's nearly three hundred words that you will never get to read.

Me: Sorry. Yeah, it is a bit late. I just need to ask a couple of questions for this story I'm doing.

Mum: Okay. Which story?

Me: The one about when I was exorcised.

Mum: Oh, you're writing about that, are you? I'm so ashamed about all that.

Me: Don't be. It's good material. Means I have something interesting to write about.

Mum: What do you want to know?

Me: Who was the priest?

Mum: [Pause] Ummm, you know, I can't remember. I think his name was Phil. Not sure of the surname.

Me: I may have to just make that up. It's not overly important anyway. Do you remember what the trigger for it was? You know, what happened that meant that I, you know, had a demon inside me?

Mum: Crikey,[22] Richard, you're not asking much, are you? Well, I seem to remember it being something to do with your asthma.

Me: My asthma? Hmmm, that's not what I remember. I have this distinct memory of it being something to do with a slice of ham.

Mum: Ham…? I don't remember that. I think it was something like they were going to exorcise the demon that was causing your asthma. You might have had an attack and it all sparked from that?

Me: I distinctly remember it being about ham.

Mum: I don't know then.

Me: Okay, I'll sort summin' out.

---

22   Although it seems unlikely that someone of sound mind would use the word 'crikey,' I promise you that not only is my mother of sound mind, she is also so awesome that she actually does use the word 'crikey.'

Mum: Anything else? Or can I go to bed?

Me: One more question. Do you remember what the actual exorcism was like? I have my version but I just wondered if you had anything I could add?

Mum: I wasn't allowed to be there. They sent me upstairs to my bedroom and I had to leave them to it. They didn't even tell me what they were going to do. I thought they were just praying for you for some reason. You're on your own with that one.

Me: They didn't let you watch? Man, that's kind of weird. I didn't realise that. It's so weird thinking back on it.

Mum: What do you mean?

Me: I don't remember it being so, kind of, strange. Like an exorcism is a pretty fucked up thing, but it didn't strike me as being such a big deal at the time.

Mum: For the sake of the story you better get on with it. This version of our conversation has shown the readers your dilemma and conveyed additional information that will add to the picture slowly forming in their minds. They know you a little bit more, so say goodnight and get on with it.

Me: Alright, night Mum.

Mum: Night darling, good luck with the story.

I don't know exactly what day it was — like so many of the 'facts' in this story, I will have to sort of wing it and make an educated guess. It was either a weekend or in some seasonal holiday, and I know this because it was late morning and I wasn't at school. I liked to snack — especially between meals. We didn't get sweets, crisps or chocolate bars as we were all a bit overweight, so my snacks consisted of savoury options such as potato salad, cheese on toast, ham and cheese toasted sandwiches, pita bread, taramasalata and hummus. Every so often I would raid the fridge and find, to my dismay, that there was nothing substantial to eat. Mum hadn't done the weekly shop so I had to improvise. And the particular day in question was one of those days.

I scanned the contents of the fridge. Sweet corn, lettuce, a jar of Coleman's wholegrain mustard, and a tub of wafer-thin honey-roasted ham. I had already checked the cupboards and they held nothing of edible significance. Fuck it, I thought,[23] ham will have to do. So I took the ham out and delved into the Perspex tub, grabbed a handful of soggy pink slices, and in true kid-who-likes-his-food-a-bit-too-much-and-

---

23   In truth, I more likely said 'Damn it,' 'How annoying,' or something thirteeny like that.

too-often fashion, I stuffed the lot in my eager mouth and began to chew. I didn't, at that very moment, realise that I had just unwittingly contracted my very own demon. Who knew you could do that? I certainly didn't.

I would love to be able to say that something extreme happened: that it suddenly went dark outside; that there was a scene-setting thunderstorm; that everything in the kitchen started shaking and rattling, drawers crashing in and out; that my eyes went completely white; that I bent over backwards and did some crazy crab-like walk up the walls (head spinning the whole three-sixty, a snake-like tongue flicking between my weirdly sharpened teeth) as I screamed FUCK YOU, FUCK YOU at no-one in particular. But I can't. Instead, while the scene hadn't changed, I had experienced a landmark epiphany: the meat was actually dead animal.

I was strangely disgusted by this realisation, to the point that I shovelled the un-swallowed ham out of my mouth with my hands. I gagged and my eyes watered in the process, but I felt somehow different, panicky. Something was wrong. The ham tasted weird. The taste remained even though it was gone, a taste of flesh. Was I some demonic carnivore? Could I eat meat again? I really liked meat. I *really* liked meat.[24] Meat was too good not to eat, but what if I couldn't? I would be torn between a desire for a nice burger and the guilt and disgust that eating one would instil in me.

I might have cried, I may have panicked and, you never know, I might even have suffered a panic-related-asthma-attack. (Telling it this way means I can be faithful to my version *and* to my Mum's retelling.) I then did what every thirteen-year-old-worrying-analytical-wimpy-kid did. I went running upstairs to Mum.

After administering motherly consolations – during which I tried, rather uselessly, to explain what was wrong – my Mum decided to make a phone call. If, in this version, I am having an asthma attack, which was a relatively common occurrence, then I would have had a small plastic mask covering my mouth, pumping sweet and sour gas into my lungs, while I tasted sweet, sweet unfettered oxygen (which is an amazing feeling, by the way – you should try it sometime).

Long story short, a conversation between our priest and my Mum played out behind closed doors, so I don't really know what was said, but I'd like to think it was short, to the point, with no pointless dialogue and no superfluous tags:

Mum: I'm worried; he's saying some strange things.

Priest: Ah, it must be a demon, possibly the devil himself.

Mum: It must be.

Priest: I will gather a circle of our close brothers and we will come and smite the

---

24   There are people who would make some kind of homo-erotic-wit-filled-comment at this point, people who would jump at the chance to say something like 'I bet you loved the meat, Rich!' So, in case you're such a person, I'll pause… …and, now that we've got that out of the way, I'll continue.

evil within the boy. No-matter what it takes, how many men we lose, we will fight the accursed beast trapped inside. It will cure him of his asthma and give him the ability to savour a good slice of ham again. Amen. [Pause] We'll be round in twenty minutes.

Mum: Lovely. I'll make us all some tea.

The next twenty minutes felt rather like the times when I did the whole ill thing on the sofa. As my Mum comforted me, I lay, burning up under my extra thick Transformers duvet, and generally felt very sorry for myself.[25] But in this case, I wasn't ill; I was possessed, and for twenty minutes I sat in silence. I didn't know what to think. *Am I possessed? There is this voice in my head. But is that just me?* I had a lot of weird, scary thoughts. But other than that, I felt pretty normal.

As with so much of this material, the exorcism itself I remember in bits and pieces. They arrived not long after they called. About twenty minutes later – fair play to the man, he wasn't late – there was a knock at the side door. All at once, six knights of God entered the house: Phil, Tim, Faith, Priest's Wife, Amanda and Jim (the latter three names are inventions. I just couldn't remember the true identities of those particular holy warriors of light). They weren't wearing robes, or armour, or anything exciting, and you're asking a lot if you think I can remember things like what they *were* wearing – we'll say clothes, maybe some jackets that they took off before having a pre-exorcism cup of tea.

Yep. First thing we did was have a good cup of tea and a chat. They asked me what was wrong. I told them. They must have done the religious-coercive-directing-towards-there-being-a-demon-in-you talk and I probably believed them, for the most part anyway. Once the possession was affirmed, we obviously had to go through all of my toys to discover the object that had drawn the demon to me in the first place.

So I directed them all to my room. I stood in the corner as they went through my room as if performing an official police search. I bit my lip and pointed out my books and toys, still unable to grasp being possessed by a demon. *What is its name? Will it speak to me? Will it speak through me? Or am I the demon?* And so it went on. They took several of my books – including about six choose-your-story-fantasy-books, which I sorely missed – a *Heroes of Might and Magic* board game and some other inconsequential items. They even tried to take my *Lord of the Rings* books. I can't quite explain how it feels to have all your favourite things taken from you in the Lord's name. It was fucking sad. I think that might actually have been the worst bit.

After we had removed the evil presences from the house, we made our way downstairs for the actual exorcism. I was shitting it. I remember that a couple of the women had a little chat on the side, in that annoying-conspiracy-God-judging way, talking about another boy who was having problems. They debated – in a reasonable way – the chance of him being possessed too.

---

25   I was a particularly unhealthy child. I suffered severe asthma attacks, itched the crap out of full body eczema, and was in and out of hospital with all kinds of ailments and wounds

Furniture was moved to create room for a circle, with space for me in the middle. The priest, Phil, got out his bible. His hair was bright white, ever so slightly wavy and perfectly shaped, as it always was. (That detail stuck out so much that I remembered it and gave that one drop of description in order that you can form an entire image for yourself; you're perfectly capable of that, or so I've been taught.) I stood in the middle of the room with my six religious elders in a circle around me. They all placed a hand on my shoulder. The priest was standing above me, clutching a bible to his dog-collared neck and chest. He placed his hand on my head, and it began.

Again there were no flashy lights, no crazy possessed screaming and flailing. Just six pretty boring people, chanting prayers – I think one attempted to get everyone into a song by humming the start, but no-one was having it and the attempt failed:

Phil: Listen to the word of God, demon. Be gone.

Me: (Internal): Erm, I don't feel anything. Is that because I'm evil? I don't know what to do. Am I supposed to be chanting and praying too? Maybe I should put my hands out, start shaking or something. Shouldn't I be doing that anyway?

Phil: Our Father... (You can insert the rest of Lord's prayer here)

Faith: (Slowly increasing the volume)yabaskibatougoukeirowrowfibedyscoobydoo[26]

Me: (Internal): Wow, this is boring. Nothing, I'm feeling nothing. Is she really speaking in tongues? It doesn't sound like any language, just the sort of gibberish I come out with when I'm trying to imitate a language. Nonsense.

Phil: In the name of God, I cast you out.

And silence. That was it. They looked pleased with themselves. I wasn't so sure. I felt pretty much the same, was still thinking about the meat thing, but now also about the being-possessed-by-a-demon thing, understandably. *Is that it? Am I forever going to be marked as an 'excorcee'? Is there some club I need to join?*

They lingered for a while in the lounge, where they all congratulated themselves, probably allowing my Mum to join us, so they could give her the good news. I sat on the couch with a glass of tropical fruit squash and pretended to be all healed, demon-free, like a child that has experienced a painful form of medical treatment. No, I'm okay, they say; I feel absolutely fine; there is no need to use that fuck off huge needle on me again. I felt the same, but I wasn't going to tell them that. I was obviously some kind of devil child, immune to God's word and forever doomed

---

26   There are no words, letters or any other ways in which I can adequately describe what someone 'speaking in tongues' sounds like. Think the Scat Man and a kid with a made-up language yodelling together on a rollercoaster.

to a life of evil. I didn't want to let them know that. I was scared.

My Mum saw them out and sat with me for a bit:

Mum: How are you feeling?

Me: The same.

Mum: Oh, darling, I'm sorry.

Me: It's okay.

Mum: Here, I got this for you.
(It was my *Lord of the Rings* Trilogy.)

Me: Yes (possibly a bit of arm pumping). Thanks Mum.

I recuperated on the couch with *The Fellowship of the Ring* and spent the afternoon fleeing from Black Riders, killing my first orc, and working up an appetite. It took me approximately two more years of doubting and questioning before I turned my back on the church, but only two hours, *Lord of the Rings*, and a healthy appetite before I enjoyed my next slice of ham.

Sitting Up / *Annamarie Scott*

I'm not sure when the tent was put up against the wall of my grandparents' house. It was one of those white paper cut-outs of a house that our school would use if it started raining and they'd wanted to put a fete on. January frost had snuck in and cracked onto the tent's plastic windows. I sat against the breakfast bar in the kitchen; behind me Mum coated bread with pâté. The tea urn hummed. Steam from the urn wafted until it collided with the yellowing ceiling and disappeared. There were bags of rolls and loaves of bread from a bakery Aunt Peggy knew, over the side and along the floor. She had arrived that morning, opened her grey car boot, and inside there were nine cellophane bags piled on one another. Someone had walked down the hill to get more meat from the corner shop; they didn't pass through the living room to get to the front door. My cereal crackled and three bread knives were sawed through fresh rolls.

I avoided the living room, just the other side of the green wall. Granddad had been in there watching her for hours, staring down at the alien thing on top of his bed. It would lie there for three days until it was carried away to St Luke's. I wasn't allowed in. I wouldn't want to see her anyway, they said.

As I had to avoid the living room, if I wanted to go upstairs I had to walk outside, beside the tent, and around to the front door, which seemed to always be on latch. During this trip, sometimes I'd be sidelined into taking a tray of tea with me to the women's tent. Inside were relatives I knew only by their faces and choices in vocabulary, who squabbled over the gossip from other trailer sites, about other relatives I didn't know.

'I'd not 'ave my girl with a gorger lad, no matter what he's like.'

'Aw, no if the boy's good to 'er then what's it matter?'

'My girl's been married to a gorger for three years. He's never laid a hand on her. Quiet boy but he dotes on her. She's happy.'

I moved my tray forward; each woman took what they wanted and continued their conversation. Occasionally a relative would look up from the white cups and look at me.

''Ere, girl. I'm your great Aunt Dolly, but if you call me 'aunt' I'll hit 'cha. If you call me 'great aunt' I'll kill ya.' She smiled around the tent. No one said anything. The electric heater hummed and a few people muttered. There were still some words I didn't know; I didn't ask for lessons or a list of terms. My sister knew all the rude Romany words by the time she was twelve. Those were the only ones she asked for.

I'd seen 'Aunt Dolly' a few times but my memory was getting hazier every day. The heater in the tent was beside her in the corner, continuing to hum under the conversations. Her folds seemed to eat up the heat before it had a chance to extend to anyone else. I sat in an empty chair, watching as my sixteen-year-old sister entered with sandwiches and then left with an empty tray. I was called in for another tea run.

The door connecting the kitchen to the living room had a window; it had only been covered by a net, but now the curtain was heavy. I imagined Granddad's bed in the living room, no mattress resting on the base. How many of them even knew her? None were from her side of the family, just in-laws. Her older sister did show up for the funeral, wearing a red coat, which wasn't received well.

The men's tent was in our neighbour's garden, though they weren't under the gazebo-esque green sheeting, but around a fire instead. The neighbour was actually my uncle, although he'd lost that title – it was a matter of principle. Their conversations, embroidered with admiration, were reconstructed from their own memories and memories of 'true' stories told to them. Exaggeration was in the family gene – my great-grandfather swore that he once helped a crashing plane by letting the nose land on the back of his Thames Trader as he drove it. I could hear the men as I went into next door's garden and approached the fire at the other end.

'He went out to the field and found the horse dead, muller'd overnight. So he props her up and goes down the pub to find old Mickey Smith and buys him a few drinks. Then he says to him, he says 'so, you still want that horse?'

'You'll sell it to me Jack?'

'Yeah well, you wanted it so much Mick, you can have the thing.' He sold the horse and when the mush went to get it the next morning it fell on him and broke his leg. Grandfather Jack was a fucker.'

I'd heard this story before. Everyone had. We had so few good ones; the best had to be re-used. Every retelling embellished the story with something more, but Grandfather Jack was a man who needed no exaggeration.

'Brush was a fucker, we were in the picture-'ouse and he lent over from behind me and says ''ere John, want a toffee?' so I took it. He'd only gone and wrapped a stone in the bloody toffee wrapper. Corr did he run, fucking broke me tooth.' The men didn't interject or talk over one another; they were a circle of friends, listening and sharing and laughing.

Taking tea to them was more comfortable, even though they stopped talking when I was near. They each thanked me and gave me a smile or a firm hand on the shoulder. I didn't realise this many family members knew I existed, let alone who my Nan was. I often greeted relatives who had no idea who I was, and spent the first five minutes of our conversation explaining my heritage while consciously dropping my 'school' accent. At other times, the pouring of tea and tearing of rolls was interrupted by the arrival of new families. When not on duty, I would clean the kitchen and venture outside to collect polystyrene cups, pushing my thumb through the bottom of each one before disposing of them.

When I went to bed, I lay and listened to the voices floating up through the window. The main bedroom was directly above the living room. If I'd fallen through the floor, I'd have landed on that mattress-less bed. I'd be inside the casket with her. I wondered how old the house was. My grandparents had been there for nearly forty years. What was the average lifespan of bedroom floorboards anyway?

Mum came upstairs to say goodnight and to apologise for being busy. Was I ok? Did I want her to stay with me a bit longer? I could stay up and wait downstairs for her if I wanted to. I don't remember answering, but she went and I stayed.

I imagined that there'd be a weight at my feet while I slept. Grandma had always sat at my feet if I'd had a hard time on a sleepover. She never told Mum if I got scared. Mum always brought up the time when I was six and I cried so much that I was brought home at midnight from my first sleepover, so I appreciated Grandma's consideration. I suppose I shouldn't have slept, or at least I shouldn't have rested. But it was as dark and hollow a sleep as I'd always had. No nightmares, no grief, just unadorned sleep.

Another day came and went on the same breeze as the last. People crowded; some from the night before went home for an hour's sleep before their nightly return. Mum always explained our family ritual as 'an Irish wake without the alcohol.' Sitting up with Nan lasted three days. My cousin was sent in to the living room, her brother and sisters kept back. She was only a year older than me. How much could I mature in a year? Was there some secret learned at ten that gave you access to a corpse?

While I took to my usual position at the breakfast bar, Mum conducted sandwich construction. The last nameless relative left with their tray while she threw broken polystyrene cups into the bin.

'I want to see Nan,' I said.

'You don't,' Mum said. I knew her opinion wouldn't have changed since the last time I'd asked. The direct approach made no difference.

'But Abbey got to.'

'Only because that shithead let her. Bastard, so-called father wouldn't let her talk to her granny when she was alive, but lets her in now.' I didn't point out that Abbey had never seemed to mind the separation from Nan, even though they lived next door.

My cousin and I made a dance routine to the entire S Club 7 album while outside in the cold. The men's gazebo-esque tent was in our garden, shielding us from the rain. A borrowed outside light interrogated us. People slipped in and out of the living room, some in groups, having conversations. They were quiet, but laughter would seep through the bricks and I wondered what joke I'd missed. I thought of Nan's red armchair – the one she used to sleep in with a green plastic milk crate under the footrest so it wouldn't fall down during the night. She'd bulk it up with nineteen pillows (I counted, one sleepover when we 'swapped beds' for the night; me on her chair, her on the brown leather sofa). Who would dare to sit in it? Her asthma and chain-smoking wasn't what led to her being brought home. Incompetent surgeons plus a cyst on her liver equalled her pink casket. I'd never seen her wear pink.

The casket arrived at Nan's house before it was sent to the funeral home. The inside only had pale pink fabric on one half of the lid. The other half exposed the metal box. For an hour and a half before her body came home, my mum and I printed, cut and pinned copies of the photographs that acted as wallpaper in Nan's living room. We covered the metal of the casket lid with the faces of friends and family and children. Everyone commented on it. Such a nice gesture – she'd loved a picture after all. No one mentioned that the pictures were on the half of the lid that covered her feet.

I got a card signed from my class, addressed to 'Anna's Nan.' A purple, sleeping face covered the front. Her head was a circle. She had a smile. Inside were condolences with the unaffected sincerity of nine-year-olds: 'I never got to meet you but I really wish I could have tried your chips.' Mum told me she would laminate it and it could go in the coffin with Nan so she could 'read it in heaven.' Her mobile was going in there too. I remember feeling relieved after learning this, just in case she was really alive and she needed us to dig her up. I asked if we should make sure it had credit but got no answer.

More relatives drifted into the tents, some venturing inside to peer into Nan's casket. I sat in the women's tent with Mum for a while. People asked if I was going back to school, if I was going to the funeral, and what flowers would be from me. Their comments included me but they never addressed me. Some people had started bringing their own children now.

Even though everyone is supposed to lose sleep when sitting up, I went to bed every night while Nan was in her coffin below me. I didn't tell anyone I was heading up, it wouldn't have made a difference to anyone anyway – they were busy with tea and flowers and funeral cars and hymns and sandwich filling. A few hours after I'd slipped upstairs Mum would always come up and sit on the bed. She'd talk to me even though I'm sure she thought I was asleep.

The final day before the funeral saw some recurring faces. Aunt Peggy, Mum and I took four sheets of plastic turf and pinned flowers to them. Mum worked on the word 'BABS,' descending in a diagonal line of pale pink rosebuds. Aunt Peggy and I fumbled with red and white carnation heads, dotting them along the eight feet of green backing. Someone must have worked on the other two sheets in the evening.

On the last night of visitor, my mum took more of an active role in the women's tent, asking about children and ill relatives. The gossip that had previously settled in the tent had been siphoned away. She thanked each woman she spoke to for coming and explained funeral arrangements to whoever asked. Flowers were the main topic of conversation; more importantly, who was having the most unique and unusual piece made. The replies from each woman didn't differ much; 'that's lovely,' they would say, or, 'ah, that's nice.'

Mum took me upstairs and showed me two pictures of myself, asking me to pick one. I chose the image of a girl with an offset smile riding a carousel horse. This was what would be put in a fame of white chrysanthemums and laid on Nan's grave from me.

'Can I see her?' I asked Mum while she put the second picture aside.

'She's not the same anymore.'

'I want to remember her face,' I said.

'She's swollen, it won't look like her anyway. We almost couldn't fit her rings on her fingers,' Mum said.

'But-'

'Enough.'

I don't remember pulling on my black blouse and trousers. Searching for my additions to the coffin is just static. A picture-memory: my hand finding a coin beneath a computer monitor (the coin needed to finish my Harry Potter collection). I stood at the door between the hallway and the living room. The window was missing, revealing six men in suits, my nineteen-year-old brother among them. This was my last chance. From the door all I could see were the tips of her slippers and the fuzz of her permed hair, but I did not step inside or go any closer. Auntie Mary turned away to cry. Mum took the silver coin and the purple-faced card. I shrugged on my coat, stood on the drive and waited for the closed, pink box to be lifted outside.

BANG BANG / *Nicolas Waddell*

The idea was to give everybody in our city a gun. One gun per person. It could be any gun: a glock, a revolver, maybe an SMG. My neighbour was given an AK. Everybody got a gun. It was a practice in National Safety being trialled in our city.

But what stopped anybody jumping in a car and driving around the city shooting up secondary schools?

I stood in a crowd of people who were all smiling and breathing heavily and jumping and waving and trying to get themselves on camera. There were screams and cheers and applause. There were mothers and their children clapping and joining the queue for collection. The Mayor smiled at us; his face was blown up on the big screens either side of him. He shook hands with the politician who'd come up with the idea. There was a close-up of the handshake and the screen froze.

'Do whatever you want with it,' they said to me after the celebrations were over and we'd filed out of the City Hall.

'Anything?'

'It's all in this leaflet here, sir. Next,' they called and moved me along. They hadn't given me any ammunition or protection; that was up to me. What the fuck was I going to do with a gun? What was anyone here going to do with a gun? It felt cold in my hands and I could see my distorted reflection in the barrel and it looked like I was smiling some twisted Joker smile. I could already smell the gunpowder.

'Is this really a good idea?'

'It's not a bad idea.'

'Oh.' No one paid me much attention. There were a lot of people there, probably about two hundred and fifty thousand: a third of the city. They were wandering around, all of them, unsupervised with fucking guns. I watched kids, no older than sixteen or seventeen, running around the Market Square pretending to shoot each other. Just pretending, just for now.

Everyone had the day off. We'd read about it in the papers and watched the news as they told us about the day's protocol. I called it Bang Bang Day. The Government had come up with some official sounding name; I think it was something like 'Experiment into the Freedom of Citizen's Self Protection Day,' which was passed under the Experiment into the Freedom of Citizen's Self Protection Act. The whole thing seemed like one of those crazy Japanese cult films called something like *Amazing Bullet Wonder Frenzy Whirlwind!*

A few years ago we were the gun crime capital of the UK.

I sat alone on the bus home. There were groups of families chatting and reading the handbooks out loud. I put my headphones in and listened to music. I could hear gunshots over guitars.

When I climbed off the bus I thanked the driver but he didn't look at me. I could see his eyes focussed on the stretch of asphalt in front of us and could see the sweat that had collected in his beard. I couldn't tell if he was armed.

I felt heavy walking home. Lopsided and weighed down. And guilty. I didn't trust anyone and they probably didn't trust me. When I was home I sat in the living room and tried to watch television but all that was on was news reports and footage from earlier in the day. They showed the Mayor and the politician and they showed the frozen handshake and they laughed. The male anchor, who used to run around in a green crocodile costume on Saturday morning television, turned to his older female co-worker and made a joke. I could see the holstered gun resting underneath his armpit, soaked with the shadow of sweat. The gun hung there unnaturally. His fingers twitched with anticipation as he faced the camera.

'The citizens of Nottingham can find all the information they need in this handbook, given to all participants.' He held up the same booklet I had. The front cover depicted a smiling family with clean haircuts and cleaner skin. They were superimposed beside the yawning lions in front of the City Hall. I could see the fountains in the background. I could see blurred images of passers-by. The newsreader turned to a different camera before it even cut and I could see his face clear in my high-definition television. His skin looked a synthetic orange under the studio lights.

He said, 'The Mayor said he hoped this would mean new and innovative things for the City of Nottingham and trusted our citizens to act accordingly. And that's all from us in the studio for today. Thank you for watching East Midlands News and have a good night.' The closing credits ran along the bottom of the screen as the studio lights dimmed.

There were already reports of disturbances the next morning. There were rumours about thirteen-year-old children shooting small animals or their best friends or their parents. Everyone blamed video games. My neighbour Phillip, the one with the AK, laughed about it. Phillip seemed like an alright guy. I didn't know what he did for a living.

'Everyone's just got to calm down, you know?' He showed me the front page of the local paper; the headline read 'Shottingham Returns.' He told me he had to go to work. After he left I went to Stonehouse's Newsagents and bought a copy of every national and local newspaper in there. *The Daily Mail* told us we were all going to Hell. *The Sun* reminded us that Katie Price was still alive. *The Guardian* reported 'Midlands City Trials Self Protection Legislation.' Everything was pretty much the same. The lonely man behind the till tried to make conversation.

'Where's your gun, son?'

'At home.' I handed him a ten pound note.

'Are you sure that's safe?'

'I only live down the road,' I said as he handed me my change. I picked up a plastic bag from the counter and slid the papers inside.

'I see. Do you want to see mine? It's beautiful.' He was smiling. Before I could reply he reached under the table and pulled out a sawn-off shotgun.

'I suppose that would be pretty effective if you get robbed,' I said. He laughed and pointed it at me. I stared, first at him, then into the two barrels of the gun pointed at my chest, then back to him.

'I'll see you later,' I said, and as I walked out the door I heard him make the sound of a gunshot.

PUHKUGHW!

When I was home and safe I spread the newspapers across my living room floor. My gun was still lying on the table next to the booklet. Neither had been moved since I'd got home yesterday. The family were still smiling and the lions were still bored. I looked through the newspapers and found an interview with this producer who was working on a new reality TV programme. I ripped it out and stuck it above my mantelpiece and tried to ignore everything while I made breakfast before work.

I walked rich people's dogs for a living, which wasn't as bad as it sounds. The money, plus tips, was enough to live pretty comfortably, and it helped me meet a lot of people and get fresh air and exercise, a bit like the dogs. But that first day was different. I got to the park with three dogs (Spud, Charley and Louis). It was half past nine and there was no one there. There wasn't even the sound of engines or children being walked to school. I hadn't seen anyone during the ten-minute walk to the park. The dogs looked at me, heads cocked as dogs do, and I shrugged.

'Don't know, guys.' I led them around the park, tried to play fetch. Their ears pointed high and their noses twitched. They moved quickly. There were no other dogs to meet and run around with. We left the park after half an hour, and when I returned them to their separate owners I was handed fifty pounds and told to leave. I didn't see anyone walking home, apart from a postman who crossed the road when he saw me.

The next morning I signed into Facebook. I saw one notification at the top of my webpage. I followed the link to a website called www.shottinghamunleashed.org. The homepage consisted of a video, underneath which was a long list of comments. I clicked play. Two kids stood talking in the street. One pulled out his gun – it looked like a Walther P99 – and shot the other in the head. There was a girl in the background. She ran up to the killer and hugged him. I re-watched the video about eight or nine times before closing down my laptop and staring up at the ceiling. It was reported in the local paper, which fell through my door later in the day, that the kids were only sixteen and had been best friends. I watched the video again at lunch and the girl stared into the camera and smiled before the footage cut out.

Phillip invited me to a party to celebrate his newfound celebrity. He was taking part in the reality TV programme. Killing Spree Reality TV. Kill or be killed, win a million. I had never been in Phillip's house before. He had IKEA shelves and IKEA sofas. His TV was big and everything was very clean. The house was full. I sat in the corner drinking warm beer and listening to the conversations around me. People compared guns and talked about the murder video and where to get cheap ammunition. They were laughing. I could hear bangs coming from the garden. I went out to get some air.

There were two people, a man and a woman, aiming their guns at a bullseye spray painted on a large dented metal sheet against Phillip's fence. They saw me and asked if I'd like to join in.

'I'm good, thanks,'

'Ah come on, sweetheart,' the woman said. She introduced herself as Karen. I'm pretty sure she was drunk. She dragged me over to where they were standing. The man said his name was Mick.

'Nice to meet you,' I said. They asked to see my gun. I'd nearly left it at home. I pulled it out of its holster, which was hidden beneath my jacket, and handed it to them.

'Beautiful. Sig Sauer .380, right?' Mick said.

I nodded. I had no idea.

He ran his finger along the barrel and pointed it at me like an action movie star. I tried to laugh. I was very aware I was breathing. I took a long swig from my warm Corona, hoping they would stop looking at me.

'Take a shot then,' said Karen. She smiled like she was once very attractive, but she looked tired and warped in the fluorescent garden lights. Mick handed me back the gun and I took aim.

Click.

Silence.

Click.

More silence.

They looked at me. Heads cocked like the dogs. I didn't want to look at them. I wished I was as drunk as Karen. Mick lit a cigarette. He walked over to me. My gun was still pointing at the target. I could feel the heat of Mick's cigarette and the smoke puffing across my face.

I thought: don't look at Mick.

I thought: go home.

But Mick wouldn't let me leave. His hand clung to my wrist and I could see the tip of the cigarette burning closer and closer to my sleeve. It had been silent for a while now. I wished I was drunk. I wished I was at home. I wished I had some ammunition.

Mick started laughing and lowered my arms for me.

'Good one,' he said. Karen was laughing too. It was a more-like a cackle.

'All out, eh?'

'Actually, I–' but Mick cut me off. He held out his gun.

'Go on,' he said, and I took it from him. It was heavier than mine. I took aim again. My eyes stung from Mick's cigarette smoke so I closed them.

I could have shot Mick.

I could have shot Karen.

I could have shot them both and ran.

I pulled the trigger. The recoil jolted my wrists and the bullet shot over the fence. My ears were ringing. I heard Mick applauding. Karen was cheering. I stared into the darkness behind the fence and wondered where the bullet might land.

The Letter / *Charlotte Zell*

She had found the perfect hideaway: The Goats' Head Arms. Inside, she went to put her bag down, but given how her Christian Louboutin shoes had stuck to the floor she thought better of it; instead, she laid out a tissue on the bar and placed her handbag on top of that.

'Whisky, neat over ice.'

The bartender poured a glass and pushed it towards her. 'On your lunch break? Fancy a look at the menu?' He peeled a laminated piece of A4 off the bar and put it down beside her. There were five options, each accompanied by a clip art representation. She swallowed the first whisky in one and pushed the glass back towards him.

'Another, please.'

He filled the glass again. 'Do you live around here? It's usually only the regulars I see.'

She looked around the pub; an older man was rubbing a ketchup spillage on his grey T-shirt, and his companion had his hand down his jogging trousers. She took another shot of her drink and the ice hit her teeth; the sharp cold and the whisky burn made her shiver.

'No, I'm not from around here.' She twisted the gold band on her left hand, rubbing it unconsciously with her thumb.

'Just visiting or business?' He was casually wiping the bar with a grimy towel.

'Funeral.'

'Oh, I'm sorry. Anyone close?' He slung the towel over his shoulder and leant in to her.

'Yes.' She rubbed the ring again and downed the rest of her drink; the ice was left clinging to the bottom of the glass. 'Another, please.'

'Can't have left you in a bad way with a rock like that.' He nodded towards the ring that she was twisting.

It was a solid gold band set with three princess-cut diamonds. She gave it another twist – the skin was becoming raw and red – then she looked down, avoiding the bartender's gaze, and stroked the rough grain of the bar. The lined wood reminded her of his hands. She remembered, years ago, before everything changed, tracing the lines on his palm; once, she had known them all. Her favourite curved around his thumb, ran fast down his palm, and joined his wrist where an old scar cut into his skin. The ink had faded, but she had still been able to make out the letters carved over his veins.

The bartender gave her a new glass with fresh ice and this time placed it on a napkin that read: 'Happy New Year, 1998!' Behind the bar, in front of the bottles, were old frosted fairy lights. She wondered if they were meant to cheer up the place, or if, like the napkins, they had been hanging around since a long-forgotten holiday. It reminded her of her eighteenth birthday; he had been so excited he had almost ripped open her gift. They had spent the night in his attic room, where small coloured lights were wrapped around the exposed beams. Instead of a proper bed he had a double mattress on the floor, and it was piled high with cushions and blankets. He had given her an original copy of *The Tale of Peter Rabbit;* it was her favourite, and he had said they would read it to their children.

Her forefinger stroked down from the ring; she traced her own lines, they were deeper now too. Her fingers ran down until they reached the gold Cartier watch that covered the red scar on the inside of her wrist. She undid the clasp, tossed the watch onto the bar and took another sip from her drink. The skin was raised, but the letters were still legible.

'That looks painful – one you did yourself?' The bartender was pretending to fold the germ-ridden towels behind the bar.

'Sort of.'

'Homemade tattoos were a brilliant thing of the eighties, weren't they?' He stuck out his hand; between his thumb and forefinger was a wonky smiley face in greenish black ink.

She half smiled but hid her wrist.

'You tossing this? Don't know many people who can afford to lose one of these.' He picked up the watch and smeared his dirty thumb across its face. He turned it over and read the inscription: 'Happy Birthday.' He chuckled and put the watch back down. 'He was obviously a rich geezer but not one of many words.'

Time didn't matter; it didn't exist here anyway. She would stay and keep drinking and the world outside this bar would keep turning; she was stuck. She had ended up where she had started. This bar – or something like it – was where she had begun. Then she thought of what she had lost; he had promised they would both get away but only she had. She had built herself anew, and the old parts she had covered up.

There was a sound of smashing glass; the bartender had dropped a bottle of Bells and it had shattered, leaving a golden puddle. She remembered the crashing plates that morning, his brother shouting that she was the one who had killed him. Unstable from grief and whisky, she tried to steady herself on the bar, but knocked the contents of her bag to the sticky floor.

She bent down to collect the fallen items. *The Tale of Peter Rabbit* had a new dent in the binding and there was an old envelope under the back cover. It was an ordinary light brown envelope on which was affixed two first class stamps.

She sat with the envelope, wondering what to do next; her manicured nail ran along its edge. She had slotted it away in the book seven years ago, but she carried it with her every day. The front of it was a mess; each stamp had a different date attached and the original address had been replaced. The handwriting was angry; it had almost cut the paper. She turned it over and the tape sealing it shut was still intact, although yellowing and peeling with age. The envelope was supposed to explain all the things she couldn't.

Behind her, a pregnant woman shoved the door open with a pushchair. Upon hearing the baby's screams, the bartender looked up from his paper and shrugged in apology. The pregnant woman looked around anyway, as though the bartender might be hiding her husband, and as she did so she bent over the pushchair and tried to pacify the baby with a cuddly toy. The tattoo on her lower back had faded algae-green.

When the pregnant woman had gone, the noise of screaming still resonated through the woman at the bar, and she felt as if she had seen her own reflection from another life. When she put a hand to her stomach, she could feel it twisting, aching from the guilt.

When they found out she was pregnant he had kissed her and promised they would get their own house and read the baby *The Tale of Peter Rabbit*. Then there was no baby.

'Need a postbox?' Bored with his paper, the bartender had sidled over.

'No, not really a letter I can send.'

'Oh, was it to–' He cut himself short. 'Was it important?'

'In a way. If he had known what was in here things might have been different.' She couldn't stop herself and the words were slurring out. 'I thought if I could read it–' She paused. 'It sounds silly.'

'Don't sound stupid to me. You need to move on and find a new man, one that can take care of you.'

Then a man entered and the door crashed closed and his footsteps knocked a rhythm on the floorboards. He stopped behind her and said, 'I'd like to settle her bill.'

She spun around, not trusting her hearing. 'What are you doing here?'

'I'm here to take you home. I knew you'd be in some hole like this.' He looked her up and down. 'Are you drunk?'

She turned and took a sip from her drink. 'I needed to come today.'

'You only think that. And how do you think this makes me feel?'

The bartender cut in. 'Is there a problem here?'

'No, this is my wife.' The man stood up taller.

The bartender looked from one to the other with his mouth hanging open. Then he carefully picked up a glass and started polishing it, looking down.

'If you want to come home with me now, I'll be outside in the car.' The man opened his leather wallet and handed over a bundle of notes. 'That should cover it.' He turned to his wife and motioned to her wrist. 'And cover that up; it looks dreadful.'

She slipped the Cartier watch back onto her wrist; it covered the scar completely. As she stood up to leave, the bartender held up the small envelope. 'Don't forget your letter.'

'It can't change anything now.' She followed her husband, leaving the envelope and everything it held in that bar.

Ava Madison / *Rea Hunt*

I'd been standing outside the Al Hirschfeld Theatre, waiting for the cast of *How To Succeed In Business Without Really Trying* to meet-and-greet with the fans, when a boy who smelled of onions shoved a card into my hand, and said 'It's going to be *the* place to be for all young talent coming into NYC – you'll meet agents, publicists, everyone basically.'

I turned the card over. As far as invitations go, this one was beautiful. Not only was the address – Nassau Street – written in cursive, gold lettering, but there was a delicate illustration of two masks – the face of comedy, and the face of tragedy. The boy, in his Jets jersey, didn't seem to match its standard.

'Seriously,' the boy said, 'it's a kosher event; it's like, sponsored by all of Broadway and stuff. How do you think so many people get into all this?' He thrust his thumb over his shoulder, indicating the Al Hirschfeld. 'You wanna be on a stage, don't you?'

I imagined Idina Menzel greeting me at the door of whatever classy venue this event was being hosted in. She'd instantly offer me a glass of champagne – expensive stuff, like vintage Dom Pérignon, not the bitter stuff I was allowed a glass of at my High School graduation party, back at my grandparents' home in Lawrence, Kansas. Idina and I would talk for hours about the time I was Dorothy in a school production of *The Wizard of Oz*, and about her stint in *Wicked*. We'd find out how much we had in common, and then she'd say, 'You know what? You'd make a perfect Elphaba. Let me introduce you to my agent.'

But there was no classy venue. There was no vintage Dom Pérignon. No glitz, no glamour, no Idina Menzel. Instead, there was an apartment. A musty, smoke-filled apartment above Caruso's Pizza and Pasta.

The first thing I saw when the onion-boy keyed open the door was a spread. The kind of spread you see at cheap proms or lacklustre funeral receptions. The table was three cupboards with a plank of wood resting haphazardly on top, covered with a lace window net that was tinged yellow in places. Empty cans of Busch and Coors Light were lolling on their sides and bottles of half-drunk Corona were left to stand by the platters and bowls of food. There were chips, dips, candy, fries and jerky everywhere. Then I saw a guy, maybe a few years older than me. He looked like he could have been an extra in *The Rocky Horror Picture Show*. His suit pants were tight and metallic silver and his hair fell to his shoulders. In one hand, he held a pot of Lay's creamy ranch dip, and in the other, four or five pretzel sticks, but he looked confused. Probably too coked-up to know what to do with them.

'You want a strawberry liquorice?' Onion-boy said, holding one out to me.

'Are you sure this is the right place?'

He nodded. His mouth was too full to speak, so he had to swallow. The noise was all saliva and spit. 'Wanna meet Strauss? He's the best agent in the city?'

'What, now? I don't kn–'

The boy grabbed me – his skinny fingers were tight around my upper arm –

and steered me into a corner of the room that was lit by a lamp with a red bulb.

Strauss was sitting on a brown loveseat couch under the lamp with an ashtray resting on his knee and a cigar trapped between his index and middle finger. He had wavy blonde hair and ginger stubble that didn't quite cover his sagging jowl. He wasn't fat, not really. It was just that jowl.

The boy stopped me in front of him. Strauss glanced at me – or rather through me, as if I wasn't there – and then he flung a little clear bag of something at the boy. 'Nice scouting, Ash. Now fuck off.'

The boy, Ash, left. I was alone with the agent.

'What's your name?'

I looked at the floor.

'Come on. Now's not the time for stage fright. What's your name?'

'Emma Matthews.'

He barked out a laugh, almost tipping over the ashtray. 'You sound like a secretary or something.'

I shrugged.

'You need a stage name. Something that's different and sexy. Ava, that's a sexy name. Like it?'

For some reason, I nodded.

'Ava...Madison? Ava Madison! That'll do. Wanna smoke?'

Strauss dug out a metal tin packed with long cigarettes and offered one to me. I didn't take it.

'Let me guess? Don't smoke?'

'I don't like it,' I said.

He shrugged and then patted the brown cushion next to him. I hesitated before taking the seat.

'Relax, Ava. You're making *me* tense.' He laughed, and then said, 'Here, just take it.'

I took the cigarette from him and sucked the smoke in from the thin end. I felt it travel to my tonsils and I expected to cough. But I didn't. Not after the second draw, or the third, either.

'See, it's not so bad, is it?' Strauss said.

I blew out more smoke as someone re-entered the room. I looked around and saw that Ash was back. He was sitting in the corner rubbing his nose. The guy with the metallic pants sat near to us now, and was joined by a girl with auburn hair and freckles. They were smiling and laughing and sharing a beer.

'Who owns this place?' I said.

'It's a dive, I know.' Strauss took the cigarette from me to smoke on himself. 'So, what are you? Actor, singer or dancer?'

'I want to be on Broadway.'

'All three then. I got Jenna Bohne the lead in *Legally Blonde* last year. She'd just moved here after graduating from Brigham.'

'I saw her. She was good!'

'Yeah.' He handed me the cigarette. It felt like my brain was starting to make weird buzzing noises, but I drew again anyway. 'She's one of my old favourites.' He took the cigarette, finished it, and then stabbed it into the ashtray, just as the front door of the apartment opened.

A girl walked in. She was wrapped up in a long coat and wore heeled boots. She greeted Strauss with a kiss on both cheeks. She was the most glitz and glamorous thing in the room, and I couldn't take my eyes off of her.

'Well, don't you just look delicious,' Strauss said.

She smiled, all white teeth, and then looked around. 'This place is still a rotting hole, I see.'

Strauss laughed. 'I've been hiding the good stuff for you.'

'Please, not that horrible champagne you used to shove down my throat?'

'You never complained before.'

'I've learnt what the *real* good stuff is since then, sweetheart.'

Strauss looked at me, but gestured at the girl. 'She's a bitch, this one is. You'll have a glass, won't you?'

I nodded. Strauss left the room then. He almost knocked his shoulder against the door frame as he walked into the kitchen and I caught a glimpse inside as the door swung. It was small and dingy. The tiles were a pattern of black and chrome.

'This is your first time here, isn't it?' the girl asked me.

I nodded again, and twisted my fingers around my other wrist. I wouldn't have noticed the action if she hadn't, and then she looked annoyed. 'You'll never make anything of yourself if you're a scared little girl all the time.'

'I'm not being a—'

'Get used to it or get out. Most people in this business are worse than a crappy room above a pizza place with a bunch of cracked-up hangers-on.' She looked at Ash, as if to prove her point. 'What's your name?'

'Emma—'

'Your *name*.'

'Ava Madison.'

'I'm Victoria Jewel.'

'I know you. You understudied as Sophie in *Mamma Mia,* right?'

'Thanks to Strauss. I just got booked for something in the works with Hugh Jackman for next year, too. He knows the director.'

'That's...' I thought it was incredible, but the idea that Strauss had done all of this didn't make sense. 'Why does he change our names?'

'Jessica Moul was a scared little girl, who would never have understudied as Sophie.'

The kitchen door swung open then and Strauss came back out with a green bottle and two tumblers. He popped the champagne cap. It didn't fizz or spurt out like champagne does in films. He poured us both a glass and placed one tumbler into my hand. He lifted his own drink up – a silent toast – and I sipped hesitantly, expecting the worst. Surprisingly, it was nice – fruity and sweet.

Ash's phone beeped. He squinted at the screen and then pulled himself up into a teetering standing position.

'Strauss,' he said, 'hey, Strauss?'

'What?'

'That was Lambert. Him and the guys just got dropped off down the street. He said they'll be here in five.'

The freckled girl that had been sitting with Rocky Horror looked over at that, and then sprung to her feet, wobbling only slightly.

Strauss checked his watch. It was a silver Rolex, and it looked real.

'Five minutes?' Freckles said. 'Strauss, let me see them. I need this.'

Strauss didn't say anything, but it looked like he was thinking hard.

'Is she OK?' I asked Victoria.

She took my glass and sipped a few mouthfuls of the alcohol, and then shoved it back into my hand. 'The cast for the new *Wicked* production sounds good, doesn't it?'

'What about Idina Menzel?'

'She's left it for that recurring role on *Glee*.'

'Oh….'

Strauss chugged from the green bottle and then called to Ash. 'Go and tidy up the bedroom, kid. Light some candles or something.'

Victoria sighed under her breath as Ash tottered into another room – the bedroom. I didn't try to see what it looked like inside; I was looking at Strauss's face as he stared at Victoria.

'What was that noise for?' he said.

'Candles won't help.'

'I'm just trying to nice it up a bit.'

'Is something the matter?' I asked.

'No,' Strauss said. 'Drink up. You've still got some champers left.' And then he walked away to grab a handful of pretzels.

'What's wrong with him?'

'That's a long list.' Victoria smiled, and then she quickly squeezed my tumbler-free hand. 'Just be Ava Madison and it'll be fine.'

Freckles came over then. She scowled at me before turning to Victoria. 'Correct me if I'm wrong, but is *she* getting contracted before *me*? She's been here five seconds. I've been waiting for this all week!'

'Back off, Cherry,' said Victoria.

Cherry looked at me again. '*I'm* getting this contract tonight, not you. I'm not missing out again, not to some talentless country farm girl.'

The front door opened without there being a knock, and three men walked in. Ash ran out of the bedroom and opened his arms in welcome. 'Mr Lambert, how are you?'

'Hey kid, you look like shit.'

Ash laughed. 'Mr Judd and, erm, Mr Donovan, can I get you anything?'

'Sit down, Ash,' Strauss said, pushing Ash away from his new guests.

He stood next to me and pulled out something from his pocket. It was the strawberry liquorice again. He offered one to me without saying anything, and I took it. We stood together eating the sweet laces as Strauss and the men talked.

'Who are they?' I said.

'Publicists.'

Lambert, Judd and Donovan walked into the bedroom.

'What the hell is going on here?'

Ash held my hand gently in his. 'This is how all the girls get started here, okay? It sucks, but they *do* get you on Broadway. It worked for Vicky and Jenna, and it'll work for you too.'

Cherry clutched at Strauss's hands. It looked like she was pleading with him to join the publicists. I understood everything then. Strauss came over, leaving Cherry with an anxious expression, and Ash transferred my hand into one of Strauss's.

'It's up to you, Ava,' Ash said.

'You can say no,' Victoria added, 'leave, and forget about all of us.'

At first, I didn't know what to say, but after a second I asked, 'This worked for you? And Jenna, right?'

Strauss nodded. 'This is way of the world, kid.'

I looked at Cherry. She looked desperate as she chewed her thumb nail. I felt that desperation too.

I nodded. It was a tiny movement of my head. Strauss didn't say anything, but he led me towards the bedroom and the three waiting publicists.

Before the door shut, I saw Victoria walk into the kitchen, and then I heard a glass fall onto the tiled floors and shatter into pieces.

Carrie / *Timothy Smith*

The lucky ones die from being too adventurous. I died almost arbitrarily during a summer's day because of someone else's decision. He was to be rewarded in heaven. I was to die and be counted. I suppose I was lucky. It was quick. A flash of light and a feeling of warmth

and then,

and then,

and then:

'I've never been here before.' He speaks but looks around. He can't make eye contact. He learnt that in school.

I'd ordered a Guinness on the long bar in the Frog and Fiddle while next to me a group of students dressed as golfers did shots. Some, later versions of themselves, were talking on mobile phones about sales deals. Outside, beyond the stickered sheet glass, a white Mercedes van was parked in front of the Asian supermarket and the same old paper-skinned smack heads were smoking at the front door. My companion, an earlier self, had ordered a bitter. Our pints poured and paid for, I'd led us outside to where, some hundred years ago, the dray had rested while the horses were fed. We'd sat on one of the benches where the sun could reach us. I'd heard myself with some friends singing Come Together on the raised wooden mezz some way off.

'I like coming here,' I say to him as I sip the first dark finger of my pint. He does the same with his bitter but says nothing. 'They did or do, I can't decide which, open readings here. For a time I would read my work to the others.'

'Are you famous?' He speaks into his pint.

'No, I just read to my friends.' He makes eye contact before turning to look at the red brick wall that the bench butts up against.

'I don't have any friends,' he states with a seasoning pride.

'That will pass.' I take another sip; pull out my tobacco, papers and lighter. I roll a cigarette. He watches my hands and then my tongue as I seal the paper around the shag.

'I smoke?'

'We do.'

'But smoking is so bad for us. You're poisoning our body.'

'I don't think that matters anymore.'

I drink and look up to the top corner of the building next to the pub. The vapour trails of all of the planes that have ever flown across Cheltenham are beginning to build up and the rumble of turbo fans is becoming a distant roar.

'I don't think there's much time left. There's an open reading today. I wanted to read to you, to everyone who has come.' I finish my cigarette and stub it out in the clean ashtray. He watches the smoke die.

'Come on, let's go inside.' I pick up my pint and he follows. We walk in, towards the dusk. The stage in the pub's function room is not much more than eighteen inches off the dark floorboards. Set around the outside is a low rail. I walk around to rear stage left. Two simple steps of chipboard and I'm up. I put my pint down and approach the microphone. I begin:

'It strikes me that within our history, and certainly within our personal history, we tell our side and, to a certain extent, we lie. In fact, I posit to you, my friends, that we lie the most when we talk about things in our immediate past.' I look at my notes, pick up my pint, take a long drink and continue.

'I think by the time we are emotionally removed enough from a triumph, disaster, or just, perhaps, a slight fuck up, we have become so distanced from those events that the fact of them is all we have left; all of the emotion has gone. If, in this age of plurality and subjectivity, the only truth is the truth of the self, then do we not lose all and find ourselves picking over the bones of something we can never change?' I pause, look up to one of the rafters, concentrate on an iron bolt and look back at my notes.

'I wanted to redress this problem. I've spent a bit of time trying to re-write a piece about a time, a fraction of our universe that meant almost all to me. I found that because of what I've said to you I couldn't do it. But, what I *can* give you is a series of moments. It is for you to do with them as you will.' I turn the page in my notes and begin:

You wear a beanie and you sit on the other side of the class with your head down low over your notes.

When you speak you play the vowels.

You are American.

You are not American but Scottish.

You have lived in the United States for the last six years.

You have worked for the Salvation Army in San Francisco.

We hold hands under the table as Dr Graham talks us through the Rwandan Genocide.

We argue over everything.

Your favourite Beatles track is 'Day in the Life.'

You are a vegetarian.

We both like Spaced.

You are afraid of underpasses.

You are always making and doing.

You cry on my shoulder after our first kiss.

You have the most perfectly round areola I have ever seen.

The first time we have sex, you look surprised, almost fight as your orgasm rises.

I've messed up and we've missed our change at Gloucester so you look at me and say: 'I like you.'

We argue and you break up with me again.

I go to work.

At the end of my shift you are there in a dress.

Your blood is on my cock because we couldn't wait.

We're warping to Cornwall and you are asleep beside me.

We walk around the Eden Project bathed in birdsong.

You say you don't sleep well without me.

We talk about who our children could be.

I crack you with a joke and it frustrates you so much you hunch like a rugby player and launch yourself at me.

I meet your family in Scotland and your Grandfather says, 'you can marry him, if you like.'

You have a nightmare about me leaving you for someone else. When you wake you are angry with me.

We're at the airport saying goodbye and you are crying.

You are crying as we talk on the phone. I don't notice.

My status on Facebook is a countdown, in minutes, until we see each other again.

I grow callous and we only talk about the sex we will have when we're reunited.

We kiss in the arrivals lounge in SF airport. I know you don't feel the same anymore.

I can't sleep so I walk down the hill to the city centre where I find us coffee and bagels.

We are shouting at each other at a wedding reception in Las Vegas.

I tell you I would marry you.

We argue on a tram to Ocean Beach. A young mother and her son move to the other end of the car.

You get me coffee and I ask you whether you were happier in the UK with me. You look out to the horizon and say 'yes.'

You thought I would hire a car and we would drive. I don't do it.

You tell me I have no right to be sad.

I phone you when I get back. It is over but you say 'don't make me cry.'

I phone you later and you tell me you have been with someone else.

I want to send you a puzzle with the words of a letter on the back of each piece.

I don't.

For fourteen months I can't watch anything about Las Vegas or San Francisco.

I try to write about you. I spend the next three years, up until my death, trying to write about you.

I finish speaking. Look out to the people gathered in the gloom and the turbine roar has reached us through the walls and the closed doors. I place my notes on the floor.

'I have reached the end of my life. I am still trying to work out what happened. I will never be happy with not knowing.' No one claps. My younger self just stares at me before there is nothing but the roar of the jets, and the endless curve of all that has come before.